青青草

中英对照

青草中英双语分级读物

些给我勇气和慧的寓言故事

第1级

总主编 林梅

本书主编 孙月英 李玉翠 于苏苏

用心灵静静感受
蕴含哲理的寓言故事

北京航空航天大学出版社
BEIHANG UNIVERSITY PRESS

图书在版编目（CIP）数据

那些给我勇气和智慧的寓言故事：汉英对照 / 林梅等主编. -- 北京：北京航空航天大学出版社，2016.4

（青青草中英双语分级读物 / 林梅主编. 第 1 级）

ISBN 978-7-5124-2077-9

Ⅰ. ①那… Ⅱ. ①林… Ⅲ. ①英语－汉语－对照读物②寓言－作品集－世界 Ⅳ. H319.4：I

中国版本图书馆 CIP 数据核字（2016）第 056402 号

青青草中英双语分级读物
——那些给我勇气和智慧的寓言故事（第1级）

总主编 林 梅

本书主编 孙月英 李玉翠 于苏苏

责任编辑 秦 莹

*

北京航空航天大学出版社出版发行

北京市海淀区学院路 37 号(邮编 100191) http://www.buaapress.com.cn

发行部电话：(010)82317024 传真：(010)82328026

读者信箱：bhwaiyu@163.com 邮购电话：(010)82316936

北京佳信达欣艺术印刷有限公司印装 各地书店经销

*

开本：787×1092 1/32 印张：9.75 字数：319 千字

2017 年 1 月第 1 版 2017 年 1 月第 1 次印刷

ISBN 978-7-5124-2077-9 定价：32.80 元

编 委 会

前　言

语言表达能力的好坏主要靠词汇量的积累，而词汇量的积累最主要的途径是阅读。研究表明：美国儿童的阅读量是中国儿童的六倍。所以想要英语好，阅读是不可忽略的关键因素。

《青青草中英双语分级读物》是一套适合小学到大学的分级阅读材料，整个套系选材考究、内容丰富多样，涵盖了童话、寓言、歌曲、电影、小说、演讲等题材，能帮助您从培养兴趣开始，循序渐进，一步一步地把您带入英语的殿堂。

配有外教真人原声录制的音频，可让您在阅读之余练习听力和跟读，也可让您进行复述、提炼和总结。这是一套能帮助您提高语言发展、阅读能力、写作能力等综合训练的工具。

这套读物的教育意义不靠说教，不靠灌输，而是渗透式、启发式的，让您在愉悦的阅读过程中学习语言、爱上阅读，并为将来的写作奠定基础。

编者

2016 年于北京

目 录

The Two Bags
两只口袋

读一读，想一想

1. 为什么人们能很快发现别人的缺点？
2. 你是否会正确认识自己，客观地评价别人？

精彩故事欣赏

1 Every man, is born into the world with two bags suspended from his neck, a bag in front full of his neighbors' faults, and a bag behind filled with his own faults. Hence it is that men are quick to see the faults of others, and yet are often blind to their own failings.

译文

1 每个人生来脖子上挂了两只口袋。前面一只装满了别人的缺点，而后面那只装的是自己的缺点。因此人们总是能够很快地看见别人的缺点，却总是看不见自己的缺点。

阅读无障碍

suspend [səˈspend] *v.* 悬挂
full of 充满
fault [fɔːlt] *n.* 缺点
fill with 装满
hence [hens] *adv.* 因此
be blind to 对……视而不见
failing [ˈfeɪlɪŋ] *n.* 短处

The Goods and the Ills

善与恶

读一读，想一想

1. 最开始，人心中的善恶比重多少？
2. 朱庇特是怎样解决善恶纠纷的？
3. 读了这个寓言故事，你学到了什么？

精彩故事欣赏

1 All the goods were once driven out by the ills from that common share which they each had in the affairs of mankind; for the ills by reason of their numbers had prevailed to possess the earth. The goods wafted themselves to heaven and asked for a righteous vengeance on their persecutors. They entreated Jupiter that they might no longer be associated with the ills, as they had nothing in common and could not live together, but were engaged in unceasing warfare, and that an indissoluble law might be laid down for their future protection.

译　文

1 善与恶原本平等地存在于人心，后来由于恶势力逐渐占据地球，所有的善都被赶出了地球。善飘荡到了天堂，申诉他们受到的压迫，渴求正义得到伸张。他们恳求朱庇特，自己要和恶一刀两断，因为他们完全不同并且水火不容。在这持久的斗争中，自己的未来应该有所保障，要有法律的保护。朱庇特答应了他们的请

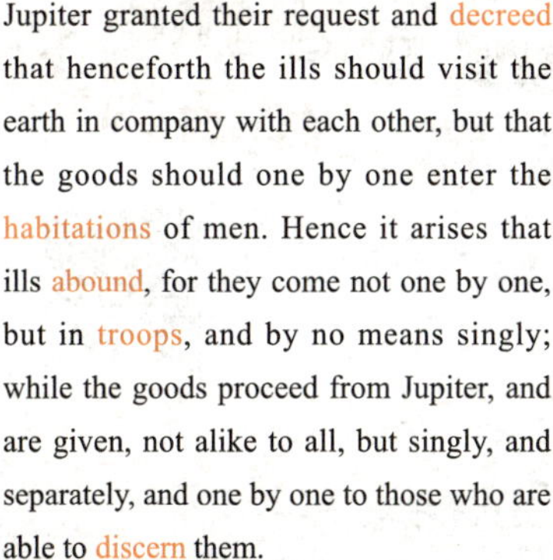

Jupiter granted their request and decreed that henceforth the ills should visit the earth in company with each other, but that the goods should one by one enter the habitations of men. Hence it arises that ills abound, for they come not one by one, but in troops, and by no means singly; while the goods proceed from Jupiter, and are given, not alike to all, but singly, and separately, and one by one to those who are able to discern them.

求，规定从此以后恶来到人间时必须成群结队，而善却要一个一个地降临人间。因此，现在恶势力总是三五成群，而不是单独存在。而善却在朱庇特的安排下单独地为那些能够分清善恶的人所拥有。

阅读无障碍

drive out 驱逐

prevail [prɪˈveɪl] v. 获胜

possess [pəˈzes] v. 主宰

waft [wɒft] v. 漂浮

righteous [ˈraɪtʃəs] adj. 公正的

vengeance [ˈvendʒəns] n. 复仇

persecutor [ˈpɜːsɪkjuːtə(r)] n. 迫害者

entreat [ɪnˈtriːt] v. 恳求

associated [əˈsəʊʃɪeɪtɪd] adj. 有关联的

unceasing [ʌnˈsiːsɪŋ] adj. 持续的

indissoluble [ˌɪndɪˈsɒljəbl] adj. 不能分解的

decreed [dɪˈkriː] v. 命令，裁定

habitation [ˌhæbɪˈteɪʃn] n. 住宅

abound [əˈbaʊnd] v. 大量存在

troop [truːp] n. 一群

discern [dɪˈsɜːn] v. 辨明，分清

The Travellers and the Plane Tree 旅人和法国梧桐

读一读，想一想

1. 旅人在马路上走的时候看见了什么？
2. 乘凉休息时，旅人是怎么谈论法国梧桐的？
3. 梧桐树认为旅人是怎样的人？

精彩故事欣赏

1 Two travellers were walking along a bare and dusty road in the heat of a summer's day. Coming presently to a plane tree, they joyfully turned aside to shelter from the burning rays of the sun in the keep shade of its spreading branches. As they rested, looking up into the tree, one of them remarked to his companion, "What a useless tree the plane is! It bears no fruit and is of no service to man at all." The plane tree interrupted him with indignation. "You ungrateful creature!" It cried: "You

译 文

1 炎热的夏日，两个旅行者顶着烈日走在空旷且尘土飞扬的马路上。不久，两人看到一棵法国梧桐树，于是高兴地坐在树荫下乘凉，躲避焦灼的阳光。在休息时，他们仰头看着头上的大树，其中一人对同伴说："这棵树真是毫无用处！结不出果子，对人类一点用都没有。"梧桐树听到后生气地打断他的话。"你们这些忘恩负义的家伙！"它吼道：

come and take shelter under me from the scorching sun, and then, in the very act of enjoying the cool shade of my foliage, you abuse me and call me good for nothing!"

"你们到我这儿来躲避太阳的暴晒，一边享受着我的叶子带给你们的阴凉，一边却骂我，说我一无是处！"

阅读无障碍

bare [beə(r)] *adj.* 光秃秃的
plane tree [plein tri:] *n.* 法国梧桐
joyfully [ˈdʒɔɪfəlɪ] *adv.* 喜悦地
ray [reɪ] *n.* 光线
shade [ʃeɪd] *n.* 阴凉处
remark [rɪˈmɑ:k] *n.* 谈论
interrupt [ˌɪntəˈrʌpt] *v.* 打断（别人的话等）
indignation [ˌɪndɪgˈneɪʃn] *n.* 愤怒
ungrateful [ʌnˈgreɪtfl] *adj.* 忘恩负义的
creature [ˈkri:tʃə(r)] *n.* 人
scorching [ˈskɔ:tʃɪŋ] *adj.* 极热的
in the very act of 正当……
foliage [ˈfəʊlɪdʒ] *n.* 植物的叶子（总称）
abuse [əˈbju:s] *v.* 辱骂

The Bee and Jupiter
蜜蜂与朱庇特

读一读，想一想

1. 为什么蜂王想要蜂针？
2. 如果蜜蜂蜇了人以后会付出怎样的代价？
3. 这个故事说明了什么道理？

精彩故事欣赏

1 A queen bee from Hymettus flew up to Olympus with some fresh honey from the hive as a present to Jupiter, who was so pleased with the gift that he promised to give her anything she liked to ask for. She said she would be very grateful if he would give stings to the bees, to kill people who robbed them of their honey. Jupiter was greatly displeased with this request, for he loved mankind; but he had given his word, so he said that stings they should have. The stings he gave them, however, were of such a kind that whenever a bee stings a

译 文

1 有只来自伊米托斯山的蜂王带着刚从蜂箱里取的新鲜蜂蜜飞到奥林匹斯山，将蜂蜜当做礼物献给了朱庇特。朱庇特很喜欢这份礼物，便答应蜜蜂满足她的任何要求。蜂王说如果能赐予蜜蜂们蜂针，在人类抢蜂蜜时能刺死他们，她将不胜感激。朱庇特对她的请求感到很生气，因为他关爱人类；但是话已经说出口了，就必须得履行，所以他还是给

man the sting is left in the wound and the bee dies.

了她蜂针。但是这蜂针却是以生命为代价的，一旦蜜蜂蜇了人，蜂针就会留在人的伤口里，而蜜蜂则会丧命。

阅读无障碍

Hymettus 伊米托斯山（希腊中东部山，雅典附近）
Olympus 奥林匹斯山
hive [haɪv] *n.* 蜂箱
promise [ˈprɒmɪs] *v.* 许诺
grateful [ˈgreɪtfl] *adj.* 感激的
sting [stɪŋ] *n.* 蜂针
rob [rɒb] *v.* 抢夺
displeased [dɪsˈpliːzd] *adj.* 生气的
give one's word 答允
wound [wuːnd] *n.* 伤口

Jupiter and the Monkey

朱庇特和猴子

读一读，想一想

1. 为什么母猴子想让小猴子参选？
2. 这个故事说明了什么？

精彩故事欣赏

1 Jupiter issued a proclamation to all the beasts of the forest and promised a royal reward to the one whose offspring should be deemed the handsomest. The monkey came with the rest and presented, with all a mother's tenderness, a flat-nosed, hairless, ill-featured young monkey as a candidate for the promised reward. A general laugh saluted her on the presentation of her son. She resolutely said, "I know not whether Jupiter will allot the prize to my son, but this I do know, that he is at least in the eyes of me his mother, the dearest, handsomest, and most beautiful of all."

译　文

1 朱庇特向森林里的所有的动物们宣布，他打算选出谁的后代最漂亮，并且赐予丰厚的奖赏。一只母猴也和其他动物一起来参选，怀里温柔地抱着一只塌鼻子、没有头发看起来病态的小猴。看到这只小猴，别的野兽哈哈大笑。而母猴眼中闪着坚定的光芒，说道："我不知道朱庇特是否会看中我的孩子，但是至少在我的眼里，我的孩子是世界上最可爱、最漂亮的。"

issue [ˈɪʃuː] *v.* 发布

proclamation [ˌprɒkləˈmeɪʃn] *n.* 宣告

royal [ˈrɔɪəl] *adj.* 盛大的

reward [rɪˈwɔːd] *n.* 赏金

offspring [ˈɒfsprɪŋ] *n.* 后代

deem [diːm] *v.* 认为

tenderness [ˈtendənɪs] *n.* 温柔

candidate [ˈkændɪdət] *n.* 候选人

salute [səˈluːt] *v.* 致意

resolutely [ˈrezəluːtlɪ] *adv.* 坚决地

allot [əˈlɒt] *v.* 分给

Jupiter and the Tortoise

朱庇特和乌龟

读一读，想一想

1. 乌龟为什么不来参加宴会？
2. 朱庇特是怎样惩罚乌龟的？

精彩故事欣赏

1 Jupiter was about to marry a wife, and determined to celebrate the event by inviting all the animals to a banquet. They all came except tortoise, who did not put in an appearance, much to Jupiter's surprise. So when he next saw the tortoise he asked him why he had not been at the banquet. "I don't care for going out," said the tortoise, "there's no place like home." Jupiter was so much annoyed by this reply that he decreed that from that time forth the tortoise should carry his house upon his back, and never be able to get away from home even if he wished to.

译　文

1 朱庇特即将娶妻，为了庆祝婚姻大事，他决定举行盛大的宴会，邀请所有动物参加。动物们纷纷前来，只有乌龟没有露面，朱庇特对此大为吃惊。于是，当他再次见到乌龟时，便问他为何没来赴宴。"我不大愿意出门，"乌龟说道，"金窝银窝不如自己的草窝。"听了乌龟的回答朱庇特勃然大怒，于是就下令，从此以后乌龟必须时刻驼着自己的家，即便想离开家也不行了。

marry [ˈmærɪ] *v.* 娶

determine [dɪˈtɜːmɪn] *v.* 决定

celebrate [ˈselɪbreɪt] *v.* 庆祝

banquet [ˈbæŋkwɪt] *n.* 宴会

except [ɪkˈsept] *prep.* 除……外

appearance [əˈpɪərəns] *n.* 出现

annoyed [əˈnɔɪd] *adj.* 恼怒的

forth [fɔːθ] *adv.* 以后

Hercules and the Wagoner

大力神和车夫

读一读，想一想

1. 车轮陷在泥潭里后车夫是怎么做的？
2. 大力神帮助车夫了吗？
3. 这个故事给我们什么启示？

精彩故事欣赏

1 A wagoner was driving a wagon along a country lane, when the wheels sank down deep into a rut. The rustic driver, stupefied and aghast, stood looking at the wagon, and did nothing but utter loud cries to Hercules to come and help him. Hercules, it is said, appeared and thus addressed him: "Put your shoulders to the wheels, my man. Goad on your bullocks, and never more pray to me for help, until you have done your best to help yourself, or depend upon it you will henceforth pray in vain."

译　文

1 一名车夫赶着货车走在一条泥泞的乡间小路上，途中车轮陷入了泥潭中。愚蠢的车夫吓得手足无措。他目瞪口呆地看着货车，大声地喊叫，祈求大力神能来帮他。大力神真的来了，却对他说：像个男人，用你的肩膀顶起车轮，用你的鞭子使劲驱赶你的牛。在你尽全力帮助自己之前，不要再向我祈祷寻求帮助。光会祈祷肯定是不管用的。

rustic [ˈrʌstɪk] *adj.* 乡下的

stupefied [ˈstjuːpɪfaid] *adj.* 目瞪口呆的

aghast [əˈgɑːst] *adj.* 吓呆的

utter [ˈʌtə(r)] *v.* 发出（声音等）

address [əˈdres] *v.* 处理

goad on 驱赶

bullocks [ˈbʊlək] *n.* 小公牛

depend upon it 毫无疑问

vain [veɪn] *adj.* 无用的

Mercury and the Sculptor

墨丘利和雕刻家

读一读，想一想

1. 墨丘利为什么装成一个凡人？
2. 墨丘利像值多少钱？
3. 从这个故事中我们可以明白什么道理？

精彩故事欣赏

1 Mercury was very anxious to know in what estimation he was held by mankind, so he disguised himself as a man and walked into a sculptor's studio, where there were a number of statues finished and ready for sale. Seeing a statue of Jupiter among the rest, he inquired the price of it. "A crown," said the sculptor. "Is that all?" said he, laughing, "and (pointing to one of Juno) how much is that one?" "That," was the reply, "is half a crown." "And how much might you be wanting for that one over there, now?" he continued, pointing to a statue of himself. "That one?" said

译　文

1 墨丘利急于想要知道自己究竟多受人类尊重，于是化成一个凡人，来到一个雕刻家的工作室，那儿有很多已经完工的雕像正准备出售。他看到其中有一尊朱庇特的雕像，便问售价是多少。"一克朗。"雕塑家说道。"就值这么多？"他笑着问道，"那么（指着朱诺——朱庇特的妻子的雕像）那尊要多少钱？""那尊？"雕塑家回答道，"要半克朗。""那

the sculptor; "Oh , I'll throw him in for nothing if you'll buy the other two."

么那边那尊雕像你要什么价呢？"他指着自己的雕像继续问道。"那尊？"雕塑家说，"哦，如果你把这两尊都买下的话，我就把它白送给你。"

阅读无障碍

anxious [ˈæŋkʃəs] *adj.* 渴望的
estimation [ˌestɪˈmeɪʃn] *n.* 尊敬
disguise [dɪsˈgaɪz] *v.* 假装
studio [ˈstjuːdɪəʊ] *n.* 工作室
a number of 许多的
statue [ˈstætʃuː] *n.* 雕像
inquire [ɪnˈkwaɪə(r)] *n.* 询问
crown [kraʊn] *n.* 克朗（5 先令的英国硬币）
throw in 附带奉送

Mercury and the Woodman

墨丘利和樵夫

读一读，想一想

1. 墨丘利给樵夫捞上来三把什么样的斧子？
2. 樵夫是一个什么样的人？
3. 在物欲横飞的现在社会，你是否有一颗知足常乐的心？

精彩故事欣赏

1 A woodman was felling a tree on the bank of a river, when his axe, glancing off the trunk, flew out of his hands and fell into the water. As he stood by the water's edge lamenting his loss, Mercury appeared and asked him the reason for his grief; and on learning what had happened, out of pity for his distress he dived into the river and, bringing up a golden axe, asked him if that was the one he had lost. The woodman replied that it was not, and Mercury then dived a second time, and, bringing up a silver axe, asked if that was his. "No, that is not mine either," said the

译　文

1 有一个樵夫正在河边砍树。突然，斧子从他的手中滑落，擦过树干，掉进了水里。当他站在水边为他掉落的斧子惋惜时，墨丘利出现了，问他为什么如此伤心。了解了事情的缘由后，出于对樵夫的同情，墨丘利跳进河里，捞上来一把金斧子问他，这是否是他掉落的那把。樵夫回答说不是。于是，墨丘利又跳进了河里，捞起一把银斧子，问他这把

woodman. Once more Mercury dived into the river, and brought up the missing axe. The woodman was overjoyed at recovering his property, and thanked his benefactor warmly; and the latter was so pleased with his honesty that he made him a present of the other two axes.

2 When the woodman told the story to his companions, one of these was filled with envy of his good fortune and determined to try his luck for himself. So he went and began to fell a tree at the edge of the river, and presently contrived to let his axe drop into the water. Mercury appeared as before, and, on learning that his axe had fallen in, he dived and brought up a golden axe, as he had done on the previous occasion. Without waiting to be asked whether it was his or not, the fellow cried, "That's mine, that's mine," and stretched out his hand eagerly for the prize, but Mercury was so disgusted at his dishonesty that he not only declined to give him the golden axe, but also refused to recover for him the one he had let fall into the stream.

是不是，“不，那把也不是我的。”樵夫回答道。墨丘利再一次跳进河里，这次捞起的正是樵夫掉落的那把斧子。看到失而复得的斧子，樵夫喜出望外，对墨丘利充满感激。墨丘利对樵夫的诚实大为赞赏，于是将另外两把斧子当成礼物送给了他。

2 当樵夫把自己的经历讲给同伴听的时候，其中一个人非常忌妒他的好运气，决定自己也去碰碰运气。于是，他也来到河边砍树，并故意把斧子掉到河里。墨丘利也和以前一样出现了，知道这个人的斧子掉在河里后，他像上次一样跳进河里捞起一把金斧子。还没等到墨丘利问他，这个人就大声叫道：“那是我的斧子，是我的。”急忙伸出手想拿到那把斧子，但墨丘利对他的不诚实感到很生气，不仅没把金斧子送给他，就连他自己丢在水中的那把也没有还给他。

阅读无障碍

glance off 擦过

lament [ləˈment] *v.* 痛惜

grief [griːf] *n.* 悲伤

distress [dɪˈstres] *n.* 不幸

property [ˈprɒpətɪ] *n.* 财物

benefactor [ˈbenɪfæktə] *n.* 恩人

contrive [kənˈtraɪv] *v.* 谋划

stretch out 伸出

decline [dɪˈklaɪn] *v.* 拒绝

recover [rɪˈkʌvə(r)] *v.* 找回

The Philosopher, the Ants, and Mercury

哲人，蚂蚁和墨丘利

读一读，想一想

1. 哲学家为什么痛斥上天不公？
2. 哲学家自己被蚂蚁咬了以后是怎么做的？
3. 我们应该如何正确对待身边的人和事？

精彩故事欣赏

1 A philosopher witnessed from the shore the shipwreck of a vessel, of which the crew and passengers were all drowned. He inveighed against the injustice of providence, which would for the sake of one criminal perchance sailing in the ship allow so many innocent persons to perish. As he was indulging in these reflections, he found himself surrounded by a whole army of ants, near whose nest he was standing. One of them climbed up and stung him, and he immediately trampled them all to death with his foot. Mercury presented

译　文

1 一个哲学家在海边目睹了一艘船遇难，所有的船员和乘客都淹死了。他痛斥上天的不公，只是因为个别罪恶的人偶然乘这艘船，竟然让这么多无辜的人都跟着陪葬。正当他为此陷入沉思时，突然发现自己站在一个蚂蚁窝边，被一大群蚂蚁围住了。有一只蚂蚁甚至爬到他脚上，咬了他一口。他立刻抬起脚把他们全踩死了。

himself, and striking the philosopher with his wand, said, "And are you indeed to make yourself a judge of the dealings of providence, who hast thyself in a similar manner treated these poor ants?"

这时，墨丘利出现了，他用权杖敲了敲哲学家说："你用相同方式对待这些可怜的蚂蚁，又怎样去评论上天的做法呢？"

阅读无障碍

shipwreck [ˈʃɪprek] *n.* 船只失事

vessel [ˈvesl] *n.* 船

inveigh [ɪnˈve] *vi.* 痛骂；谩骂

injustice [ɪnˈdʒʌstɪs] *n.* 不公正；不讲道义

providence [ˈprɒvɪdəns] *n.* 天道

sake [seɪk] *n.* 缘由

perchance [pəˈtʃɑːns] *adv.* 偶然

perish [ˈperɪʃ] *v.* 死亡

indulge [ɪnˈdʌldʒ] *v.* 沉溺于

trample [ˈtræmpl] *v.* 踩踏

strike [strɪk] *v.* 敲打

wand [wɒnd] *n.* 权杖

hast [hæst] *v.* 有（have 的第二人称单数现在式）

thyself [ðaɪˈself] pro*n.* 你自己（用作第二人称单数反身代词）

The Rich Man and the Tanner 有钱人与制皮匠

读一读，想一想

1. 有钱人为什么让制皮匠搬走？
2. 制皮匠最终搬走了吗？
3. 这个故事说明了什么？

精彩故事欣赏

1 A rich man took up his residence next door to a tanner, and found the smell of the tan-yard so extremely unpleasant that he told him he must go. The tanner delayed his departure, and the rich man had to speak to him several times about it, and every time the tanner said he was making arrangements to move very shortly. This went on for some time, till at last the rich man got so used to the smell that he ceased to mind it, and troubled the tanner with his objections no more.

译 文

1 一个有钱人与一个制皮匠比邻而居。他实在受不了制皮匠院子里传出的气味，便让皮匠搬家。制皮匠一再拖延搬家日期，有钱人说了好几次让他快点搬家，制皮匠每次都说马上就搬，却一拖再拖，始终没有搬走。一段时间以后，有钱人习惯了皮革的气味，就不再为难皮匠了。

阅读无障碍

residence [ˈrezɪdəns] *n.* 住宅

smell [smel] *n.* 气味

tan-yard [ˈtænjˈɑːd] *n.* 制革工场

delay [dɪˈleɪ] *v.* 推迟

departure [dɪˈpɑːtʃə(r)] *n.* 离开

several [ˈsevrəl] *adj.* 几个的

cease [siːs] *v.* 停止

objection [əbˈdʒekʃn] *n.* 反对

The Image of Mercury and the Carpenter

墨丘利像和木匠

读一读，想一想

1. 木匠为什么供奉着墨丘利的雕像？
2. 木匠的供奉得到回报了吗？
3. 故事的结局说明了什么？

精彩故事欣赏

1 A very poor man, a carpenter by trade, had a wooden image of Mercury, before which he made offerings day by day, and begged the idol to make him rich, but in spite of his entreaties he became poorer and poorer. At last, being very angry, he took his image down from its pedestal and dashed it against the wall. When its head was knocked off, out came a stream of gold, which the carpenter quickly picked up and said, "Well, I think thou art altogether contradictory and unreasonable; for when I paid you honor, I reaped no

译　文

1 一个贫穷的木匠供奉着一个墨丘利的木雕像，每天都会在雕像前摆上贡品，祈求墨丘利能让他发财。尽管他日日祈求，日子却每况愈下。最后，一怒之下他将神像从供桌上拿下来狠狠地摔到墙上。神像的头被摔断了，大量金子从里面涌出，木匠连忙拾起神像，说道："我觉得你简直是不可理喻。我之前一直尊敬你，供奉你，

benefits; but now that I maltreat you I am loaded with an abundance of riches."

却得不到好处；现在对你不好，你反倒使我发了横财。"

阅读无障碍

by trade 就职业而言
offering [ˈɒfərɪŋ] *n.* 贡品
in spite of 尽管……
entreaty [ɪnˈtriːtɪ] *n.* 恳求
pedestal [ˈpedɪstl] *n.* 供桌
dash [dæʃ] *v.* 猛掷
contradictory [ˌkɒntrəˈdɪktəri] *adj.* 矛盾的
maltreat [ˌmælˈtriːt] *v.* 虐待
an abundance of 丰富的

The Bald Huntsman

秃头的猎人

读一读，想一想

1. 猎人秃头后是怎么做的？
2. 他打猎时发生了什么？
3. 他最后的话说明一个什么道理？

精彩故事欣赏

1 A man who had lost all his hair took to wearing a wig, and one day he went out hunting. It was blowing rather hard at the time, and he hadn't gone far before a gust of wind caught his hat and carried it off, and his wig too, much to the amusement of the hunt. But he quite entered into the joke, and said, "Ah, well! the hair that wig is made of didn't stick to the head on which it grew, so it's no wonder it won't stick to mine."

译文

1 有个人的头发掉光了，就戴了一顶假发。一天，他出去打猎，突然，一阵狂风吹来，他没走远把他头上的帽子和假发一起吹跑了，一下子成了猎人中的笑料。这个人反而自嘲道："哈哈，好吧，制成这顶假发的那些头发，在原主人的头上都待不住，所以难怪它们也无法待在我的头上。"

阅读无障碍

wig [wɪg] *n.* 假发
rather [ˈrɑːðə(r)] *adv.* 相当
gust [gʌst] *n.* 一阵狂风
amusement [əˈmjuːzmənt] *n.* 消遣
stick to 保留
no wonder 难怪

Mercury And the Tradesmen

墨丘利和商人

读一读，想一想

1. 为什么商人都会说谎？
2. 为什么马贩子最会说谎？

精彩故事欣赏

1 When Jupiter was creating man, he told Mercury to make an infusion of lies and to add a little of it to the other ingredients which went to the making of the tradesmen. Mercury did so, and introduced an equal amount into each in turn-the tallow-chandler, and the greengrocer, and the haberdasher, and all, till he came to the horse-dealer, who was last on the list, when, finding that he had a quantity of the infusion still left, he put it all into him. This is why all tradesmen lie more or less, but they none of them lie like a horse-dealer.

译　文

1 朱庇特创造人类时，吩咐墨丘利制造一点让人说谎的药，并把它加进其他材料里，于是造出了商人。墨丘利按照要求依次平均把说谎药加到每种生意人身上——蜡烛商、菜贩子，杂货商等等。最后轮到了名单上的最后一种商人马贩子。这时墨丘利却发现还剩下很多药，于是，他便将所有剩余的药全部加在马贩子身上。这正是为什么商人多少都会说谎，而马贩子却尤为突出。

infusion [ɪn'fju:ʒn] *n.* 注入物

ingredient [ɪn'gri:diənt] *n.* 原料

introduce [ˌɪntrə'dju:s] *v.* 引进

tallow-chandler ['tæləu 'kændl ə] *n.* 蜡烛商

greengrocer ['gri:ngrəusə(r)] *n.* 菜贩

haberdasher ['hæbədæʃə(r)] *n.* 杂货商

a quantity of 一些

The Astronomer
天文学家

读一读，想一想

1. 一天晚上天文学家观察星星时发生了什么意外？
2. 谁救了天文学家？
3. 那个施救者最后的话事什么意思？

精彩故事欣赏

1 An astronomer used to go out at night to observe the stars. One evening, as he wandered through the suburbs with his whole attention fixed on the sky, he fell accidentally into a deep well. While he lamented and bewailed his sores and bruises, and cried loudly for help, a neighbor ran to the well, and learning what had happened said: "Hark ye, old fellow, why, in striving to pry into what is in heaven, do you not manage to see what is on earth?"

译 文

1 有位天文学家习惯晚上出去观察星星。一天晚上，当他正走在郊外聚精会神地观察天空时，一不小心掉进一口井里。他疼痛难忍，一边查看自己的伤口一边大声呼救。附近的人听到呼救声就赶了过来。当弄明白情况后，便对他说："喂，老兄，你整天把心思都用在观察天上的东西了，现在连地上的东西也看不清了？"

suburb [ˈsʌbɜːb] *n.* 郊区

accidentally [æksɪˈdentəlɪ] *adv.* 意外地

well [wel] *n.* 井

lament [ləˈment] *v.* 悲伤

bewail [bɪˈweɪl] *v.* 悲叹

sore [sɔː(r)] *n.*（肌肤的）痛处

bruise [bruːz] *n.* 瘀伤

strive [straɪv] *v.* 努力奋斗

pry [praɪ] *v.* 窥探

Hercules and Plutus
赫拉克勒斯和财神

读一读，想一想

1. 宙斯为什么设宴？
2. 赫拉克勒斯是怎样对待财神的？
3. 这个小故事有什么启示？

精彩故事欣赏

1 When Hercules was received among the gods and was entertained at a banquet by Jupiter, he responded courteously to the greetings of all with the exception of Plutus, the god of wealth. When Plutus approached him, he cast his eyes upon the ground, and turned away and pretended not to see him. Jupiter was surprised at this conduct on his part, and asked why, after having been so cordial with all the other gods, he had behaved like that to Plutus. "Sire, " said Hercules, "I do not like Plutus, and I will tell you why, When we were on earth together I always noticed that he was

译　文

1 赫拉克勒斯被接纳成为神以后，朱庇特设宴为他庆贺。宴会上赫拉克勒斯亲切地向众神问好，唯独没理会财神普罗托斯。当财神向他走过来时，他低下头看着地面，然后转身走开了，假装没看到他。朱庇特对他的行为感到非常惊讶，刚才他那么热诚地和别的神打招呼，现在竟然如此对待财神普罗托斯，于是就问他为什么。"陛下，"赫拉克勒斯回

to be found in the company of scoundrels."

答说："我不喜欢普罗托斯，这是有原因的。当我们俩都在人间时，我总会见到他与坏人在一起。"

阅读无障碍

entertain [ˌentəˈteɪn] *v.* 款待
courteously [ˈkɜːtɪəslɪ] *adv.* 亲切地
with the exception of 除……以外
approach [əˈprəʊtʃ] *v.* 走近
pretend [prɪˈtend] *v.* 假装
conduct [kənˈdʌkt] *n.* 行为
cordial [ˈkɔːdiəl] *adj.* 热诚的
scoundrel [ˈskaʊndrəl] *n.* 坏蛋

The Peacock And Juno

孔雀和朱诺

读一读，想一想

1. 为什么孔雀向朱诺抱怨？
2. 朱诺是怎样向孔雀解释的？
3. 这个故事说明了什么道理？

精彩故事欣赏

1 The peacock was greatly discontented because he had not a beautiful voice like the nightingale, and he went and complained to Juno about it. "The nightingale's song," said he, "is the envy of all the birds, but whenever I utter a sound I become a laughing-stock." The goddess tried to console him by saying, "You have not, it is true, the power of song, but then you far excel all the rest in beauty: your neck flashes like the emerald and your splendid tail is a marvel of gorgeous color." But the peacock was not appeased. "What is the use," said he, "of being

译　文

1 孔雀因为自己没有夜莺那样美妙的歌喉而非常不满，于是去找朱诺抱怨。"夜莺美妙的歌声，"她说，"是所有鸟类都嫉妒的，而我却一开口，就会成为大家的笑料。"女神朱诺尽力安慰他道："你在唱歌方面的确不占优势，但是你的容貌确是任何其他鸟类所无法比拟的：你的脖子像绿宝石一样的荧光闪闪，你那开屏的尾巴更是光彩照人。"可是孔雀仍

beautiful, with a voice like mine?" Then Juno replied, with a shade of sternness in her tones, "Fate has allotted to all their destined gifts: to yourself beauty, to the eagle strength, to the nightingale song, and so on to all the rest in their degree, but you alone are dissatisfied with your portion. Make, then, no more complaints. For, if your present wish were granted, you would quickly find cause for fresh discontent."

旧不满足。"声音那么难听，"孔雀说，"长得美丽又有什么用呢？"朱诺用微微严肃的语气回应道："命运赋予了每个人不同的礼物——你非凡的美貌，老鹰强大的力量，夜莺优美的歌喉等等，所有生命都与众不同，各有所长。只有你对自己所拥有的不满足。不要再抱怨了，因为如果你现在的愿望得到了满足的话，你很快又会找新的不满足的借口。"

阅读无障碍

discontented [ˌdɪskənˈtentɪd] *adj.* 不满意的
nightingale [ˈnaɪtɪŋgeɪl] *n.* 夜莺
complain [kəmˈpleɪn] *vi.* 抱怨
laughing-stock [ˈlaːfɪŋ stɒk] *n.* 笑柄
goddess [ˈgɒdes] *n.* 女神
console [kənˈsəʊl] *v.* 安慰
excel [ɪkˈsel] *v.* 优于
emerald [ˈemərəld] *n.* 绿宝石
splendid [ˈsplendɪd] *adj.* 华丽的
marvel [ˈmɑːvl] *n.* 奇异的事物
gorgeous [ˈgɔːdʒəs] *adj.* 光彩夺目的
sternness [ˈstəːnɪs] *n.* 严厉
destined [ˈdestɪnd] *adj.* 命中注定的
portion [ˈpɔːʃn] *n.* 部分

The Salt Merchant and His Ass 盐商与他的驴

读一读，想一想

1. 盐商赶着驴子过河时发生了什么？
2. 盐商是怎样对付驴子的小把戏的？
3. 驴子最后自食其果给我们什么警示？

精彩故事欣赏

1 A peddler drove his Ass to the seashore to buy salt. His road home lay across a stream into which his ass, making a false step, fell by accident and rose up again with his load considerably lighter, as the water melted the sack. The peddler retraced his steps and refilled his panniers with a larger quantity of salt than before. When he came again to the stream, the ass fell down on purpose in the same spot, and, regaining his feet with the weight of his load much diminished, brayed triumphantly as if he had obtained what he desired. The peddler saw through his trick and drove

译　文

1 一个盐商赶着驴子去海边买盐。回来的路上经过一条小河，驴子失足跌到了水里去。等重新站起来时，发现驴背上的担子减轻了许多，原来是因为水把袋子里的盐溶解了。盐商又回去重新买了更多的盐。当他又回到小河边过河时，驴子故意在老地方摔倒，再爬起来时，他的担子果然又减轻了，驴子达到了目的得意扬扬地直叫。盐商看穿了它的

him for the third time to the coast, where he bought a cargo of sponges instead of salt. The ass, again playing the fool, fell down on purpose when he reached the stream, but the sponges became swollen with water, greatly increasing his load. And thus his trick recoiled on him, for he now carried on his back a double burden.

诡计就决定教训它。于是又赶着驴子第三次来到海边，这次盐商没买盐而是买了一大包海绵。再次来到河边，驴子故计重施，又故意跌进水里。结果海绵吸饱了水，担子的重量大大加重了。驴子自食其果，最终驮着双倍的重量回去。

阅读无障碍

considerably [kən'sɪdərəbli] *adv.* 非常

sack [sæk] *n.* 麻袋

retrace [rɪ'treɪs] *v.* 折回

pannier ['pæniə(r)] *n.* 驮筐

on purpose 故意地

regain [rɪ'geɪn] *v.* 重新获得

diminished [dɪ'mɪnɪʃt] *adj.* 减少了的

bray [breɪ] *v.* 发出驴叫声

triumphantly [traɪ'ʌmfəntlɪ] *adv.* 得意洋洋地

obtain [əb'teɪn] *v.* 获得

sponge [spʌndʒ] *n.* 海绵

instead of 代替

recoil [rɪ'kɔɪl] *v.* 报应

burden ['bɜːdn] *n.* 重担

Hercules and Minerva
赫拉克勒斯和密涅瓦

读一读，想一想

1. 赫拉克勒斯见到那个苹果大小的东西时怎么做的？
2. 赫拉克勒斯最后为什么不知所措了？
3. "天下本无事，庸人自扰之"符合这篇文章的主旨吗？

精彩故事欣赏

1 Hercules was once traveling along a narrow road when he saw lying on the ground in front of him what appeared to be an apple, and as he passed he stamped upon it with his heel. To his astonishment, instead of being crushed it doubled in size, and, on his attacking it again and smiting it with his club, it swelled up to an enormous size and blocked up the whole road. Upon this he dropped his club, and stood looking at it in amazement. Just then Minerva appeared, and said to him, "Leave it alone, my friend, that which you see before you is the apple of discord: if you do not meddle

译 文

1 有一次赫拉克勒斯在一条狭窄的小路上行走，看到地上有个像苹果大小的东西。他经过时就用脚去踩它，突然，让他吃惊的是那东西没被踩碎反而变大了两倍。于是，他更加用力去踩，还用木棒狠敲。结果那东西越胀越大，最后把路都堵住了。直到这时赫拉克勒斯扔下木棒，不知所措地站在那里看着这一切。这时，密涅瓦出现了，对他说道：

with it, it remains small as it was at first, but if you resort to violence it swells into the thing you see."

"伙计，别管它了。如果你不去理它的话，它不过苹果大小，结果你与它争斗，现在却连路都过不去了。"

stamp [stæmp] *v.* 用脚踩踏

to one's astonishment 令人吃惊的是

crush [krʌʃ] *v.* 压破

smite [smaɪt] *v.* 重击

club [klʌb] *n.* 棍棒

swell [swel] *v.* 膨胀

enormous [ɪˈnɔːməs] *adj.* 巨大的

block up 堵塞

in amazement 吃惊地

discord [ˈdɪskɔːd] *n.* 不和

meddle [ˈmedl] *v.* 干预

resort to violence 用暴力

The Man and the Satyr

旅人和萨堤罗斯

读一读，想一想

1. 那个人为什么把手放在嘴边吹气？
2. 他为什么又对着盘子吹气？
3. 这个故事告诉我们什么为人处世的道理？

精彩故事欣赏

1 A man and a Satyr having struck up an acquaintance, sat down together to eat. The day being wintry and cold, the man put his fingers to his mouse and blew upon them. "What's that for, my friend?" asked the Satyr. "My hands are so cold," said the man, "do it to warm them." In a little while some hot food was placed before them, and the man, raising the dish to his mouse, again blew upon it. "And what's the meaning of that, now?" said the Satyr. "Oh," replied the man, "my porridge is so hot, I do it to cool it." "Nay, then," said the

译 文

1 一个人偶然间结识了萨堤罗斯，两人坐在一起吃东西。正值冬天，天寒地冻，于是那人把手放在嘴边哈气。"我的朋友，那是干什么？"萨堤罗斯问道。"我的手太冷了，"这人说道，"这样做的话手就暖和了。"过了一会儿，一些热腾腾的食物上桌了，那人又把盘子举到嘴边吹了起来。"这又是干什么？"萨堤罗斯问，

Satyr, "from this moment I renounce your friendship, for I will have nothing to do with one who blows hot and cold with the same mouse."

"哦"那人答道，"我的粥太烫了，我把它吹得凉一点"。萨堤罗斯说："从今往后我们一刀两断，因为我不想有一个反复无常的朋友。"

strike up 建立

acquaintance [ə'kweɪntəns] *n.* 相识

wintry ['wɪntrɪ] *adj.* 冬天的

renounce [rɪ'naʊns] *v.* 断绝关系

The Traveler and Fortune
旅人和命运女神

读一读，想一想

1. 旅人为什么倒在井边？
2. 命运女神为什么把旅人叫醒？
3. 当你做错事的时候，是从自身查找原因还是怨天尤人？

精彩故事欣赏

1 A traveler wearied from a long journey lay down, overcome with fatigue, on the very brink of a deep well. Just as he was about to fall into the water, Dame Fortune, it is said, appeared to him and waking him from his slumber thus addressed him: "Good Sir, pray wake up: for if you fall into the well, the blame will be thrown on me, and I shall get an ill name among mortals; for I find that men are sure to impute their calamities to me, however much by their own folly they have really brought them on themselves."

译文

1 有个旅行者经过长途跋涉后，筋疲力尽，倒在一口深井边睡着了。就在他快要掉下井去的时候，命运女神出现了，把他叫醒了。女神对他说："朋友，请你醒一醒。万一你不小心掉下了井，一定会责怪我，我将因此在人间背负一个坏名声。因为我发现，虽然实际上人们是由于自己的愚蠢而招来灾祸，却总是把不幸归罪于我。"

weary [ˈwiərɪ] *v.* 疲倦

fatigue [fəˈtiːg] *n.* 疲劳

brink [brɪŋk] *n.*（危险的）边沿；

slumber [ˈslʌmbə(r)] *n.* 熟睡

blame [bleɪm] *n.* 责备

impute [ɪmˈpjuːt] *v.* 归咎于

calamity [kəˈlæmətɪ] *n.* 灾祸

folly [ˈfɒlɪ] *n.* 蠢笨

Prometheus and the Making of Man

普罗米修斯与造人

读一读，想一想

1. 普罗米修斯创造了什么？
2. 朱庇特发现人和动物数量差距大时又下了什么命令？
3. 为什么有些人是人面兽心？

精彩故事欣赏

1 At the bidding of Jupiter, Prometheus set about the creation of man and the other animals. Jupiter, seeing that mankind, the only rational creatures, were far outnumbered by the irrational beasts, bade him redress the balance by turning some of the latter into men. Prometheus did as he was bidden, and this is the reason why some people have the forms of men but the souls of beasts.

译　文

1 普罗米修斯遵从朱庇特的命令，创造了人类和其他动物。朱庇特看到毫无理性的动物在数量上远远超过了有理性的人类，于是又命令他把其中一些动物变成人，以使两者达到平衡。普罗米修斯执行了朱庇特的命令。因此，有些人有着人的外形，却是动物的内心。

阅读无障碍

bidding [ˈbɪdɪŋ] *n.* 命令

creation [kriˈeɪʃn] *n.* 创造

rational [ˈræʃnəl] *adj.* 理性的

outnumber [ˌaʊtˈnʌmbə(r)] *v.* 数量多于

irrational [ɪˈræʃənl] *adj.* 无理性的

redress [rɪˈdres] *v.* 改正

balance [ˈbæləns] *n.* 平衡

The Witch

女巫

读一读，想一想

1. 女巫为什么被判死刑?
2. 这个故事告诉我们一个什么道理?

精彩故事欣赏

1 A witch professed to be able to avert the anger of the gods by means of charms, of which she alone possessed the secret; and she drove a brisk trade, and made a fat livelihood out of it. But certain persons accused her of black magic and carried her before the judges, and demanded that she should be put to death for dealings with the devil. She was found guilty and condemned to death. And one of the judges said to her as she was leaving the dock, "You say you can avert the anger of the gods. How comes it, then, that you have failed to disarm the enmity of men?"

译 文

1 有个女巫声称自己能念咒语，平息神明的愤怒。她经常并且只有她自己知道这个秘诀以此招摇撞骗，收敛了一大笔财富。但后来有人控告她使用巫术，做邪恶交易，把她抓去见法官，要求判她死刑。女巫被判有罪并处以死刑。一个法官在她即将离席被押赴刑场时问她："你既然声称能平息神明的愤怒，那为什么现在，连人类的愤怒都平息不了呢？"

avert [ə'vɜːt] *v.* 避免

by means of 用

charm [tʃɑːm] *n.* 咒语

possess [pə'zes] *v.* 拥有

brisk [brɪsk] *adj.* 兴隆的

livelihood ['laɪvlɪhʊd] *n.* 生计

dock [dɒk] *n.* 被告席

disarm [dɪs'ɑːm] *v.* 使息怒

enmity ['enmətɪ] *n.* 怨恨

The Old Man and Death

老人与死神

读一读，想一想

1. 老人为什么呼唤死神？
2. 老人真的想让死神把他带走吗？
3. 我们应该怎样对待生命？

精彩故事欣赏

1 An old man was gathering sticks in a forest. At last he grew very tired and hopeless. He threw down all the sticks and cried out, "I cannot bear this life any longer. Ah, I wish Death would come and take me!" As he spoke, Death appeared, and said to him, "What would you do, old man? I heard you call me." "Please, sir," replied the old man, "would you help me lift this bundle of sticks up to my shoulder?"

译文

1 一个老人在森林中砍了不少柴，十分吃力地挑着走了很远的路。最后他累极了，实在挑不动了，于是放下担子，大喊起来，"我再也受不了这种日子了，死神啊，求你把我带走吧。"正说着，死神来了，对他说，"老人家，你想做什么，我听见你叫我？""先生，"老人答道，"您能帮忙将这捆柴放在我的肩上吗？"

gather ['gæðə(r)] *v.* 收集

bear [beə(r)] *v.* 忍受

bundle ['bʌndl] *n.* 一捆

The Rogue and the Oracle

无赖和圣人

读一读，想一想

1. 无赖打算怎样证明圣人是不可信的？
2. 圣人是怎样回应无赖的？
3. 这个故事说明什么道理？

精彩故事欣赏

1 A rogue laid a wager that he would prove the oracle at Delphi to be untrustworthy by procuring from it a false reply to an inquiry by himself. So he went to the temple on the appointed day with a small bird in his hand, which he concealed under the folds of his cloak, and asked whether what he held in his hand were alive or dead. If the oracle said "dead," he meant to produce the bird alive; if the reply was "alive," he intended to wring its neck and show it to be dead. But the oracle was one too many for him, for the answer he

译　文

1 一个无赖和别人打赌说他能证明德尔菲的圣人是不可信的，他提出的问题圣人会给出错误的答案。于是到了约定的日子，他来到神庙，手里攥着一只小鸟，并把手藏在外衣的褶皱里。他问圣人自己手里的东西是活的还是死的。如果圣人说"是死的"，他就直接把活鸟拿出来；如果说"是活的"，他就悄悄扭断小鸟的脖子再

got was this: "Stranger, whether the thing that you hold in your hand be alive or dead is a matter that depends entirely on your own will."

把死的拿出来。然而，圣人远比他更胜一筹，他回答道："陌生人，不管你手中拿的东西是死还是活，这完全取决于你自己的意愿。"

阅读无障碍

rogue [rəʊg] *n.* 无赖
wager [ˈweɪdʒə(r)] *n.* 打赌
untrustworthy [ʌnˈtrʌstwɜːði] *adj.* 不能信赖的
procure [prəˈkjʊə(r)] *v.* 获得
inquiry [ɪnˈkwaɪərɪ] *n.* 询问
appointed [əˈpɔɪntɪd] *adj.* 约定的
conceal [kənˈsiːl] *v.* 遮住
fold [fəʊld] *n.* 褶皱
one too many for 胜人一筹
entirely [ɪnˈtaɪəlɪ] *adv.* 完全地

The Farmer and the Snake

农夫与蛇

1. 农夫为什么把蛇揣到怀里？
2. 蛇是怎么报答农夫的？
3. 农夫的悲惨遭遇给我们什么警示？

精彩故事欣赏

1 One winter, a farmer found a snake stiff and frozen with cold. He had compassion on it, and taking it up, placed it in his bosom. The snake was quickly revived by the warmth, and resuming its natural instincts, bit its benefactor, inflicting on him a mortal wound. "Oh," cried the farmer with his last breath, "I am rightly served for pitying a scoundrel."

译文

1 在一个寒冷的冬日，一个农夫看见一条蛇冻僵了。他觉得它很可怜，就把蛇拾起来，小心翼翼地揣进怀里。蛇温暖后，很快苏醒了过来，恢复了它的本性，咬了它的恩人一口，使他受到了致命的创伤。农夫临死前痛悔地说："天哪！我竟然同情坏人，结果反而遭到这样的报应。"

阅读无障碍

stiff [stɪf] *adj.* 僵硬的
frozen [ˈfrəʊzn] *adj.* 冻硬的
compassion [kəmˈpæʃn] *n.* 同情
bosom [ˈbʊzəm] *n.* 胸口
revived [rɪˈvaɪvd] *adj.* 复活的
warmth [wɔːmθ] *n.* 温暖
resume [rɪˈzjuːm] *v.* 恢复
instinct [ˈɪnstɪŋkt] *n.* 本能
benefactor [ˈbenɪfæktə(r)] *n.* 恩人
inflict [ɪnˈflɪkt] *v.* 伤害
mortal [ˈmɔːtl] *adj.* 致命的
wound [waʊnd] *n.* 伤口
served [sɜːv] *v.* 对待
pity [ˈpɪtɪ] *v.* 怜悯
scoundrel [ˈskaʊndrəl] *n.* 恶棍

The Laborer and the Snake

农工和蛇

1. 农夫为什么要杀死蛇？
2. 为什么蛇不与农工和解？
3. 这个寓言说明了什么道理？

精彩故事欣赏

1 A snake, having made his hole close to the porch of a cottage, inflicted a mortal bite on the cottager's infant son. Grieving over his loss, the father resolved to kill the snake. The next day, when it came out of its hole for food, he took up his axe, but by swinging too hastily, missed its head and cut off only the end of its tail. After some time the cottager, afraid that the snake would bite him also, endeavored to make peace, and placed some bread and salt in the hole. The snake, slightly hissing, said: "There can henceforth be no

译 文

1 一条毒蛇在一户农舍门廊附近打洞藏身。一天，它爬出来咬死了农夫幼小的儿子。农夫悲痛万分，一心要杀死蛇报仇。第二天，当蛇从蛇洞爬出来觅食时，农夫一斧头就朝蛇砍去，可惜砍得太匆忙，没砍到蛇头，只是砍掉一小截蛇尾。过了一会，农夫担心蛇也会咬自己，便在蛇洞旁放了些面包和盐，试图与蛇和解。蛇发

peace between us; for whenever I see you I shall remember the loss of my tail, and whenever you see me you will be thinking of the death of your son."

出嘶嘶的响声，说道："从此以后我们势不两立；我一见到你就想起被砍掉的尾巴，同样，你一见到我就会想起你那死去的儿子。"

阅读无障碍

porch [pɔːtʃ] *n.* 门廊
cottage [ˈkɒtɪdʒ] *n.* 小屋
inflict [ɪnˈflɪkt] *v.* 使遭受
infant [ˈɪnfənt] *adj.* 幼小的
grieve [griːv] *v.* 哀伤
resolve [rɪˈzɒlv] *v.* 决定
hastily [ˈheɪstɪlɪ] *adv.* 匆忙地
endeavor [ɪnˈdevə] *v.* 试图
hiss [hɪs] *v.* 发嘶嘶声

Farmer and the Cranes
农夫和鹤

读一读，想一想

1. 鹤来麦田觅食，农夫是怎么应对的？
2. 农夫见投石器不起作用后又是怎么做的？
3. 这个故事说明了什么？

精彩故事欣赏

1 Some cranes made their feeding grounds on some plowlands newly sown with wheat. For a long time the farmer, brandishing an empty sling, chased them away by the terror he inspired, but when the birds found that the sling was only swung in the air, they ceased to take any notice of it and would not move. The farmer, on seeing this, charged his sling with stones, and killed a great number. The remaining birds at once forsook his fields, crying to each other, "It is time for us to be off to Liliput, for this man is no longer

译　文

1 一些鹤来到一片刚播种的麦田里觅食。农夫见他们很久不散，于是就设置了一些投石器吓唬他们。可是不久这些鹤就发现投石器只是在风中摆动而没什么大作用，就不再理会这些投石器，照样在麦田找种子吃。见此情景，农夫就把投石器上安上了石子，结果打死了很多鹤。剩下的鹤这才赶紧离开麦田，互相告诫道，“我

content to scare us, but begins to show us in earnest what he can do."

们赶紧离开这里吧，看起来这人不是单纯的吓唬我们了，这次是动真格的了。"

plowland [ˈplaʊˌlænd] *n.* 田地
sow [səʊ] *v.* 播种
wheat [wiːt] *n.* 小麦
brandish [ˈbrændɪʃ] *v.* 挥舞
sling [slɪŋ] *n.* 投石器
chase [tʃeɪs] *v.* 驱逐
terror [ˈterə(r)] *n.* 恐怖
inspire [ɪnˈspaɪə(r)] *v.* 激发
cease [siːs] *v.* 停止
charge [tʃɑːdʒ] *v.* 装载
remaining [rɪˈmeɪnɪŋ] *adj.* 剩下的
forsake [fəˈseɪk] *v.* 放弃
in earnest 认真地

The Ploughman and the Wolf 农夫和狼

读一读，想一想

1. 狼为什么要吃牛轭上的皮带子？
2. 狼头卡住后他是怎么做的？
3. 从这个故事中我们能得到什么道理？

精彩故事欣赏

1 A ploughman loosed his oxen from the plough, and led them away to the water to drink. While he was absent a half-starved wolf appeared on the scene, and went up to the plough and began chewing the leather straps attached to the yoke. As he gnawed away desperately in the hope of satisfying his craving for food, he somehow got entangled in the harness, and, taking fright, struggled to get free, tugging at the traces as if he would drag the plough along with him. Just then the ploughman came back, and seeing what was happening, he cried,

译 文

1 农夫解下拉犁的牛，牵着它们去水边喝水。他刚走，一只饿得半死的狼出现了，狼走到犁旁，吃起了牛轭上的皮带子。为了填饱肚子，狼拼命地啃着皮套，不知不觉就把头伸进了牛轭中结果出不来了，狼拼命挣扎着想重获自由却没有用，只好拉着犁跑，就像要去田里耕地似的。这时农夫回来了，看到眼前发生的一切，

"Ah, you old rascal, I wish you would give up thieving for good and take to honest work instead."

便喊道："啊，你这老坏蛋，但愿你放弃偷东西，靠劳动自食其力。"

plough [plaʊ] *n.* 犁
absent [ˈæbsənt] *adj.* 不在场的
half-starved [ˌhɑːfˈ stɑːvd] *adj.* 半饿半饱的
scene [siːn] *n.* 现场
chew [tʃuː] *v.* 咀嚼
leather [ˈleðə(r)] *n.* 皮革
strap [stræp] *n.* 带子
attached [əˈtætʃt] *adj.* 附加的
yoke [jəʊk] *n.* 牛轭
gnaw [nɔː] *v.* 啃咬
desperately [ˈdespərətlɪ] *adv.* 不顾一切地
satisfy [ˈsætɪsfaɪ] *v.* 满足
entangle [ɪnˈtæŋgl] *v.* 陷入
harness [ˈhɑːnɪs] *n.* 轭具
fright [fraɪt] *n.* 惊吓
struggle [ˈstrʌgl] *v.* 挣扎
tug [tʌg] *v.* 用力拉
trace [treɪs] *n.* 痕迹
drag [dræg] *v.* 拖拽
rascal [ˈrɑːskl] *n.* 坏蛋
thieve [θiːv] *v.* 偷

The Farmer and His Sons
农夫和他的儿子们

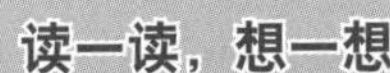

1. 农夫离世前有什么心愿？
2. 农夫为什么说葡萄园里有宝物？
3. 真正的宝物是什么？

精彩故事欣赏

1 A father, being on the point of death, wished to be sure that his sons would give the same attention to his farm as he himself had given it. He called them to his bedside and said, "My sons, there is a great treasure hid in one of my vineyards." The sons, after his death, took their spades and mattocks and carefully dug over every portion of their land. They found no treasure, but the vines repaid their labor by an extraordinary and superabundant crop.

1 有个农夫很快就要离开人世了，他希望儿子们能和他一样精心照料农场。他把儿子们叫到床边，说："孩子们，在我的葡萄园里埋着一大笔宝物。"父亲去世之后，儿子们拿上铁锹和锄头把那葡萄园的地全都翻了一遍又一遍，可是什么宝物都没找到，却使葡萄园的地变得很松软。到了秋天，葡萄获得了巨大的丰收。

阅读无障碍

attention [əˈtenʃn] *n.* 照料
treasure [ˈtreʒə(r)] *n.* 金银财宝
vineyard [ˈvɪnjəd] *n.* 葡萄园
spade [speɪd] *n.* 铁锹
mattock [ˈmætək] *n.* 锄头
portion [ˈpɔːʃn] *n.* 一部分
labor [ˈleɪbə(r)] *n.* 劳动
extraordinary [ɪkˈstrɔːdnri] *adj.* 非凡的
superabundant [ˌsjuːpərəˈbʌndənt] *adj.* 极多的

The Snake and Jupiter
蛇和朱庇特

读一读，想一想

1. 蛇为什么抱怨？
2. 朱庇特教蛇怎样做？
3. 这个故事说明了什么？

1 A snake suffered a good deal from being constantly trodden upon by man and beast, owing partly to the length of his body and partly to his being unable to raise himself above the surface of the ground. So he went and complained to Jupiter about the risks to which he was exposed. But Jupiter had little sympathy for him. "I dare say," said he, "that if you had bitten the first that trod on you, the others would have taken more trouble to look where they put their feet."

1 一条蛇由于身体过长且无法离开地面而饱受被人类和野兽践踏的痛苦。于是，他去向朱庇特抱怨自己暴露在危险中。但是朱庇特却并不同情他。“我敢说，”朱庇特说道：“如果你把第一个践踏你的人咬伤的话，其他人再走路时一定会仔细看清落脚点。”

tread [tred] *v.* 践踏

risk [rɪsk] *n.* 危险

expose [ɪkˈspəʊz] *v.* 暴露

sympathy [ˈsɪmpəθi] *n.* 同情

take the trouble to 不怕麻烦去做

The Wasps, the Partridges, and the Farmer

黄蜂，鹧鸪和农夫

读一读，想一想

1. 黄蜂和鹧鸪是怎样向农夫求水喝的？
2. 农夫为什么宁愿把水给牛喝？
3. 生活中会说重要还是会做更重要？

精彩故事欣赏

1 The wasps and the partridges, overcome with thirst, came to a farmer and besought him to give them some water to drink. They promised amply to repay him the favor which they asked. The partridges declared that they would dig around his vines and make them produce finer grapes. The wasps said that they would keep guard and drive off thieves with their stings. But the farmer interrupted them, saying: "I have already two oxen, who, without

译 文

1　一群黄蜂和鹧鸪口渴难忍，飞到农夫那里求水喝。他们许诺一定会报答农夫的善行。鹧鸪声称他们会给葡萄园松土，以便结出累累硕果。黄蜂许诺说会守护葡萄园，用毒刺赶走来偷葡萄的贼。但是农夫打断了他们的话："我已经有两头牛了，他们什么活都能干，却

making any promises, do all these things. It is surely better for me to give the water to them than to you."

从不许诺什么。因此，我宁愿把水给他们喝，而不是给你们。"

wasp [wɒsp] *n.* 黄蜂
partridge [ˈpɑːtrɪdʒ] *n.* 鹧鸪
overcome [ˌəʊvəˈkʌm] *v.* 受不了
beseech [bɪˈsiːtʃ] *v.* 恳求
amply [ˈæmplɪ] *adv.* 充足地
declare [dɪˈkleə(r)] *v.* 声称

The Two Men Who Were Enemies 两个仇人

读一读，想一想

1. 两个死对头上船以后是怎么做的？
2. 为什么其中一个说死而无憾了？
3. 这个小故事说明了什么？

精彩故事欣赏

1 Two men, deadly enemies to each other, were sailing in the same vessel. Determined to keep as far apart as possible, the one seated himself in the stern, and the other in the prow of the ship. A violent storm arose, and with the vessel in great danger of sinking, the one in the stern inquired of the pilot which of the two ends of the ship would go down first. On his replying that he supposed it would be the prow, the man said: "Death would not be grievous to me, if I could only see my enemy die before me."

译 文

1 有两个死对头同乘一艘船航行。两人决意离得越远越好，一个坐在船尾，另一个坐在船头。突然海上起了大风暴，船眼看就要沉了，船尾的那个人就问领航员，船的哪一部分会先沉没。领航员说他估计应该是船头先沉。那人于是说："能看见我的死对头先我而死，我死而无憾了。"

vessel ['vesl] *n.* 船
stern [stem] *n.* 船尾
prow [praʊ] *n.* 船首
arise [ə'raɪz] *v.* 出现
pilot ['paɪlət] *n.* 引航员
grievous ['griːvəs] *adj.* 令人伤心或痛苦的

The Horse and the Groom

马和马夫

读一读，想一想

1. 马夫是怎样对待他的马的？
2. 马是怎样对马夫说的？
3. 马夫是个怎样的人？

精彩故事欣赏

1 A groom used to spend whole days in currycombing and rubbing down his horse, but at the same time stole his oats and sold them for his own profit. "Alas!" said the horse, "if you really wish me to be in good condition, you should groom me less, and feed me more."

译　文

1 从前有个马夫整天给他的马梳理皮毛、擦洗，但同时却为了自己利益把喂马的燕麦偷走卖掉了，"唉！"马叹了口气，对马夫说："如果你真心想要我膘肥体壮的话，你不必整天给我梳洗，而应该多给我喂些饲料。"

阅读无障碍

currycomb [ˈkʌriːkəʊm] *v.* 用马梳梳

rub down 擦身

oat [əʊt] *n.* 燕麦

profit [ˈprɒfɪt] *n.* 收益

alas [əˈlæs] int.（表示悲痛、遗憾）哎呀

in good condition 身体状况好

groom [gruːm] *v.* 清洁

The Herdsman and the Lost Bull

牧人和丢失的公牛

读一读，想一想

1. 谁偷走了小公牛？
2. 牧羊人丢了牛后是怎么发誓的？
3. 牧羊人发现真的偷牛贼后又是怎么做的？

精彩故事欣赏

1 A herdsman tending his flock in a forest lost a bull-calf from the fold. After a long and fruitless search, he made a vow that, if he could only discover the thief who had stolen the calf, he would offer a lamb in sacrifice to Hermes, Pan, and the Guardian Deities of the forest. Not long afterwards, as he ascended a small hillock, he saw at its foot a lion feeding on the calf. Terrified at the sight, he lifted his eyes and his hands to heaven, and said: "Just now

译文

1 有个牧人在树林中放牛，丢了一头小公牛。他四处找了很久，结果白费力气。于是他发誓，如果能找到偷牛贼，他愿意为森林守护神赫尔墨斯和潘神献上一只羊。很快，当他爬上一座小山丘时，忽然看见山脚下有只狮子正在吃他的小牛。牧人被眼前所见的景象吓坏

I vowed to offer a lamb to the Guardian Deities of the forest if I could only find out who had robbed me, but now that I have discovered the thief, I would willingly add a full-grown bull to the calf I have lost, if I may only secure my own escape from him in safety."

了，急忙仰望天空，举手祷告："我刚才发誓，如果捉到偷牛贼，我愿供奉一只羊给森林守护神。现在我已经找到了那个贼，除了那只小牛外，我愿意再添上一只大牛，只要能让我安全逃离狮子。"

阅读无障碍

tend [tend] *v.* 照看
bull-calf [ˈbʊlkˈɑːf] *n.* 小公牛
fold [fəʊld] *n.* 队伍
fruitless [ˈfruːtləs] *adj.* 徒劳的
vow [vaʊ] *n.* 誓言
discover [dɪˈskʌvə(r)] *v.* 发现
sacrifice [ˈsækrɪfaɪs] *n.* 献祭
Guardian Deities 守护神
ascend [əˈsend] *v.* 攀登
hillock [ˈhɪlək] *n.* 小丘
willingly [ˈwɪlɪŋlɪ] *adv.* 愿意地
full-grown [ˈfulˈgrəun] *adj.* 成熟的
secure [sɪˈkjʊə(r)] *v.* 保护
escape [ɪˈskeɪp] *v.* 逃脱

The Goat and the Goatherd

山羊和牧羊人

读一读，想一想

1. 牧羊人为什么打断了羊角？
2. 山羊最后的话说明了什么？

1 A goatherd had sought to bring back a stray goat to his flock. He whistled and sounded his horn in vain, the straggler paid no attention to the summons. At last the goatherd threw a stone, and breaking its horn, begged the Goat not to tell his master. The goat replied, "Why, you silly fellow, the horn will speak though I be silent."

译 文

1 一个牧羊人赶着羊群往回走，有一只山羊落在后面，根本没注意他的召唤的口哨声。于是牧羊人扔了一块石头过去，正巧打断了一只羊角。牧羊人吓得求山羊不要将此事告诉主人。山羊却说："即使我不说，又怎能隐瞒下去呢？难道主人看不出我的角断了吗？"

seek [siːk] *v.* 寻找

stray [streɪ] *adj.* 走失的

flock [flɒk] *n.* 羊群

horn [hɔːn] *n.* 哨声

vain [veɪn] *adj.* 徒劳的

summon [ˈsʌmən] *n.* 召唤

horn [hɔːn] *n.* 角

silent [ˈsaɪlənt] *adj.* 沉默的

The Goatherd and the Wild Goats

牧羊人和野山羊

读一读，想一想

1. 牧羊人为什么喂野山羊更多的饲料？
2. 野山羊为什么不留下来？
3. 我们应该怎样对待自己的老朋友？

精彩故事欣赏

1 A goatherd, driving his flock from their pasture at eventide, found some wild goats mingled among them, and shut them up together with his own for the night. The next day it snowed very hard, so that he could not take the herd to their usual feeding places, but was obliged to keep them in the fold. He gave his own goats just sufficient food to keep them alive, but fed the strangers more abundantly in the hope of enticing them to stay with him

译 文

1 傍晚，一个牧羊人赶着他的羊群放牧归来。他发现有几只野山羊混在羊群中，于是就把它们和自己的羊关在一起过夜。第二天，下起了大雪，牧羊人没法带着羊群去它们以往吃草的地方放牧了，只好让羊群待在羊圈里。他只给自己的羊刚刚能填饱肚子的饲料，却用

and of making them his own. When the thaw set in, he led them all out to feed, and the wild goats scampered away as fast as they could to the mountains. The goatherd scolded them for their ingratitude in leaving him, when during the storm he had taken more care of them than of his own herd. One of them, turning about, said to him: "That is the very reason why we are so cautious: for if you yesterday treated us better than the goats you have had so long, it is plain also that if others came after us, you would in the same manner prefer them to ourselves."

大量的草喂那几只野山羊，希望以此引诱它们留下来，成为他自己的羊。冰雪融化后，牧羊人把羊都放出来吃草，那些野山羊立刻冲出羊群，向山上跑去。牧羊人生气地大骂，责怪它们忘恩负义离他而去，说暴风雪期间自己对它们照顾地比自己的羊还好。其中一只野山羊听到后，转过头来对他说："这正是我们小心提防你的原因：昨天你对我们比对那些跟了你那么长时间的羊都好，很显然，如果以后又有羊加入进来的话，你又会同样地去冷落我们而只偏爱他们。"

阅读无障碍

pasture [ˈpɑːstʃə(r)] *n.* 牧场
eventide [ˈiːvntaɪd] *n.* 黄昏
mingle [ˈmɪŋgl] *v.* 混进
herd [hɜːd] *n.* 牧群
be obliged to 不得不
sufficient [səˈfɪʃnt] *adj.* 足够的
abundantly [əˈbʌndəntli] *adv.* 大量地
entice [ɪnˈtaɪs] *v.* 引诱
thaw [θɔː] *n.* 解冻时节
scamper [ˈskæmpə(r)] *v.* 奔跑
scold [skəʊld] *v.* 责骂
ingratitude [ɪnˈgrætɪtjuːd] *n.* 忘恩负义
cautious [ˈkɔːʃəs] *adj.* 小心的
plain [pleɪn] *adj.* 明显的
manner [ˈmænə(r)] *n.* 做法

The Shepherd and the Sea

牧羊人和海

读一读，想一想

1. 牧羊人为什么要做海上生意?
2. 牧羊人是怎样逃生的?
3. 牧羊人对过路人说的话是什么意思?

1 A shepherd, keeping watch over his sheep near the shore, saw the sea very calm and smooth, and longed to make a voyage with a view to commerce. He sold all his flock, invested it in a cargo of dates, and set sail. But a very great tempest came on, and the ship being in danger of sinking, he threw all his merchandise overboard, and barely escaped with his life in the empty ship. Not long afterwards when someone passed by and observed the unruffled calm of the sea, he interrupted him and said: "It is again in want of dates, and therefore looks quiet."

1 有个牧羊人总是在海边放羊，看见大海风平浪静，就想去海上做生意赚钱。于是他卖掉了羊群，买了一船冬枣出发了。不料途中遇到了暴风雨，船经受不住，眼看就要沉没了。没办法，他只好忍痛把所有货物都抛到海里，这才乘坐着空船幸免于难。不久之后，有人路过此地，看着平静的大海，这时，牧人走过去对他说："它又想要枣子了，所以才会看起来如此宁静。"

long [lɒŋ] *v.* 渴望

voyage [ˈvɔɪɪdʒ] *n.* 航行

commerce [ˈkɒmɜːs] *n.* 贸易

invest [ɪnˈvest] *v.* 购买

cargo [ˈkɑːgəʊ] *n.*（轮船、飞机所装载的）货物

date [deɪt] *n.* 海枣

tempest [ˈtempɪst] *n.* 暴风雨

merchandise [ˈmɜːtʃəndaɪs] *n.* 货物

overboard [ˈəʊvəbɔːd] *adv.* 向船外

observe [əbˈzɜːv] *v.* 观察

unruffled [ʌnˈrʌfld] *adj.* 平静的

interrupt [ˌɪntəˈrʌpt] *v.* 打断（别人的话等）

The Shepherd and the Wolf 牧羊人和狼

读一读，想一想

1. 牧羊人教狼干什么坏事？
2. 狼学会偷东西后是怎么对牧羊人说的？
3. 这个故事说明什么？

精彩故事欣赏

2 A shepherd once found the whelp of a wolf and brought it up, and after a while taught it to steal lambs from the neighboring flocks. The wolf, having shown himself an apt pupil, said to the shepherd: "Since you have taught me to steal, you must keep a sharp lookout, or you will lose some of your own flock."

译 文

2 有一次，一个牧羊人捡到一只小狼崽，就把它带回家养大了，然后教它去偷附近的小羊羔。小狼崽为了显示自己是个聪明的学生，就对牧羊人说："既然你教会了我偷东西，那你一定要看好自己的羊，不然也许哪天你的羊也会丢失。"

阅读无障碍

whelp [welp] *n.* 幼兽
steal [stiːl] *v.* 偷
neighboring [ˈneɪbərɪŋ] *adj.* 邻近的
apt [æpt] *adj.* 聪明的
sharp [ʃɑːp] *adj.* 敏锐的
lookout [ˈlʊkaʊt] *n.* 警戒

The Shepherd and the Dog

牧羊人和狗

读一读，想一想

1. 牧羊人把什么赶进了羊圈？
2. 如果狗没有发现狼，会有什么后果？
3. 这个故事给我们什么启示？

1 A shepherd penning his sheep in the fold for the night was about to shut up a wolf with them, when his dog perceiving the wolf said: "Master, how can you expect the sheep to be safe if you admit a wolf into the fold?"

1 傍晚，牧羊人把羊群赶进羊圈正准备将一只狼与羊群混在一起关起来，他的狗发现羊群中藏着一只狼，赶紧对牧羊人说："主人，你把一只狼放进了羊圈，还怎么能指望羊群的安全呢？"

阅读无障碍

pen [pen] *v.* 把……关入栏中

perceive [pə'siːv] *v.* 察觉

shut up 关门

The Shepherd and the Sheep 牧羊人和羊

读一读，想一想

1. 牧羊人见到满树的橡子后是怎么做的？
2. 羊吃了什么？
3. 从这个故事中我们明白一个什么道理？

精彩故事欣赏

1 A shepherd driving his sheep to a wood, saw an oak of unusual size full of acorns, and spreading his cloak under the branches, he climbed up into the tree and shook them down. The sheep eating the acorns inadvertently frayed and tore the cloak. When the Shepherd came down and saw what was done, he said, "Oh you most ungrateful creatures! You provide wool to make garments for all other men, but you destroy the clothes of him who feeds you."

译　文

1 牧羊人赶着一群绵羊来到树林里，看见一棵高大的橡树上结满了橡子。牧羊人便把外衣脱下来铺在树枝上，然后爬上树，使劲摇晃，橡子纷纷落地。他的绵羊尽情享用着这些橡子，不知不觉把牧羊人的外衣也咬坏了。牧人从树上下来后，见此情形非常生气，大骂道："你们这些狼心狗肺的东西！你们把羊毛给别人做衣服穿，却把辛苦喂养你们人的外衣糟蹋了。"

acorn [ˈeɪkɔːn] *n.* 橡子

spread [spred] *v.* 展开

cloak [kləʊk] *n.* 外套

branch [brɑːntʃ] *n.* 树枝

inadvertently [ˌɪnədˈvɜːtəntli] *adv.* 疏忽地

fray [freɪ] *v.* 磨损

tear [teə(r)] *v.* 撕裂

ungrateful [ʌnˈgreɪtfl] *adj.* 忘恩负义的

garment [ˈgɑːmənt] *n.* 衣服

The Hunter and the Woodman

猎人和樵夫

读一读，想一想

1. 猎人在森林中干什么？
2. 你是一个真正勇敢的人吗？

1 A hunter, not very bold, was searching for the tracks of a Lion. He asked a man felling oaks in the forest if he had seen any marks of his footsteps, or if he knew where his lair was. "I will," he said, "at once show you the Lion himself." The hunter, turning very pale, and chattering with his teeth from fear, replied, "No, thank you. I didn't ask that, it is his track only I am in search of, not the Lion himself."

1 有个胆小的猎人，正在搜寻一只狮子的踪迹。他问一个在森林中砍橡树的樵夫，有没有见过狮子的足迹，或知道狮子的巢穴在哪里。樵夫说："我可以立刻把你带到狮子那里去。"猎人一听，吓得脸色苍白，牙齿打战地说："不用了，谢谢你。我只是在寻找它的足迹，并不想找狮子本身。"

bold [bəʊld] *adj.* 勇敢的
search [sɜːtʃ] *v.* 搜寻
track [træk] *n.* 踪迹
fell [fel] *v.* 砍倒
oak [əʊk] *n.* 橡树

footstep [ˈfʊtstep] *n.* 足迹
lair [leə(r)] *n.*（野兽的）巢穴
pale [peɪl] *adj.* 苍白的
chatter [ˈtʃætə(r)] *v.* 打颤
fear [fɪə(r)] *n.* 害怕

The Hunter and the Horseman 猎人和骑手

读一读，想一想

1. 骑手是怎样得到兔子的？
2. 猎人追上骑手了吗？
3. 猎人是一个真正慷慨的人吗？

1 A certain hunter, having snared a hare, placed it upon his shoulders and set out homewards. On his way he met a man on horseback who begged the hare of him, under the pretense of purchasing it. However, when the horseman got the hare, he rode off as fast as he could. The hunter ran after him, as if he was sure of overtaking him, but the horseman increased more and more the distance between them. The hunter, sorely against his will, called out to him and said, "Get along with you! For I will now make you a present of the hare."

1 有个猎人打了一只兔子，扛着兔子往家走。路上他遇到一个骑马的人。那个人看到他便停下来假装要买兔子。然而骑马的人一拿到兔子，就纵马飞奔而去。猎人在后面拼命地追赶，但终究没追上，骑手离他越来越远。望着渐渐远去的骑马的人，猎人无可奈何地大喊："你走吧！那只兔子送给你了。"

snare [sneə(r)] *v.* 捕捉
homewards [ˈhəʊmwədz] *adv.* 向家
pretense [prɪˈtens] *n.* 假装
purchase [ˈpɜːtʃəs] *v.* 购买
overtake [ˌəʊvəˈteɪk] *v.* 赶上

increase [ɪnˈkriːs] *v.* 增加
distance [ˈdɪstəns] *n.* 距离
sorely [ˈsɔːli] *adv.* 严重地
will [wɪl] *n.* 愿意

The Fowler and the Viper
捕鸟者和蝰蛇

读一读，想一想

1. 蝰蛇为什么咬了捕鸟人一口？
2. 捕鸟人的悲惨结局给我们一个什么警示？

精彩故事欣赏

2 A fowler, taking his bird-lime and his twigs, went out to catch birds. Seeing a thrush sitting upon a tree, he wished to take it, and fitting his twigs to a proper length, watched intently, having his whole thoughts directed towards the sky. While thus looking upwards, he unknowingly trod upon a viper asleep just before his feet. The viper, turning about, stung him, and falling into a swoon, the man said to himself, "Woe is me! that while I purposed to hunt another, I am myself fallen unawares into the snares of death."

译 文

2 一个捕鸟人，带着粘鸟胶和杆子出去捕鸟。他看见树上有只画眉，就想捉住它。于是他把粘鸟杆子调好合适的长度，全神贯注地盯着天空。当他专注于天空的时候，他不知不觉的踩到一条在他脚前睡觉的蝰蛇。蝰蛇转身咬了他一口。他渐渐失去知觉，自言自语道："我真倒霉！我想捕捉别的猎物的时候，却丝毫不知自己已经落入死亡的圈套中了。"

bird-lime [ˈbɜːdlˈaɪm] *n.* 粘鸟胶
twig [twɪg] *n.* 小树枝
thrush [θrʌʃ] *n.* 画眉鸟
proper [ˈprɒpə(r)] *adj.* 适当的
intently [ɪnˈtentlɪ] *adv.* 专心地
directed [dɪˈrektɪd] *adj.* 定向的
tread [tred] *vi.* 踩
viper [ˈvaɪpə(r)] *n.* 蝰蛇
swoon [swuːn] *n.* 昏倒
woe [wəʊ] *n.* 灾难
purpose [ˈpɜːpəs] *v.* 企图（做）
unawares [ˌʌnəˈweəz] *adv.* 出其不意地
snare [sneə(r)] *n.* 圈套

The Fowler, the Partridge, and the Cock
捕鸟人、鹧鸪和公鸡

读一读，想一想

1. 捕鸟人为什么要杀鹧鸪？
2. 捕鸟人为什么放了鹧鸪杀了公鸡？
3. 这个故事有什么启示？

1 One day, as a fowler was sitting down to a scanty supper of herbs and bread, a friend dropped in unexpectedly. The larder was empty, so he went out and caught a tame partridge, which he kept as a decoy, and was about to wring her neck when she cried, "Surely you will kill me? Why, what will you do without me next time you go fowling? How will you get the birds to come to your nets?" He let her go at this, and went to his hen-house, where he had a plump young cock. When the

1 一天晚餐时间，捕鸟人正坐在餐桌旁吃着家里仅有的香草和面包，一个朋友不期而至。食品橱里什么吃的也没了，于是捕鸟人出去捉住了自己驯养的那只鹧鸪，那是他用来当诱饵捕鸟的。就在捕鸟人要拧断她的脖子时，鹧鸪喊道："你确定要杀了我吗？为什么？如果没有我，下次你怎么捕

cock saw what he was after, he too pleaded for his life, and said, "If you kill me, how will you know the time of night, and who will wake you up in the morning when it is time to get to work?" The fowler, however, replied, "You are useful for telling the time, I know, but, for all that, I can't send my friend supperless to bed." And therewith he caught him and wrung his neck.

鸟？你怎样吸引鸟进入你的网里？”听到鹧鸪的话，捕鸟人就放了她，然后来到鸡舍，要捉里面那只肥胖的公鸡。公鸡看到自己成为下一个目标，赶紧苦苦哀求主人饶命，并且说：“如果你杀死我，你怎么能知道晚上的时间呢？谁又能在早晨叫你起床干活呢？”然而，捕鸟人却回答道：“我知道，你的确能报时，可是我也不能让我的朋友不吃晚饭饿着肚子睡觉啊。”随后，他捉住公鸡，拧断了他的脖子。

阅读无障碍

scanty [ˈskænti] *adj.* 勉强够的

herb [hɜːb] *n.* 香草

drop in 顺便拜访

unexpectedly [ˌʌnɪkˈspektɪdlɪ] *adv.* 未料到地

larder [ˈlɑːdə(r)] *n.* 食物橱

tame [teɪm] *adj.* 驯服的

decoy [ˈdiːkɔɪ] *n.* 诱饵

fowl [faʊl] *v.* 捕鸟

plump [plʌmp] *adj.* 肥胖的

supperless [ˈsʌpəlɪs] *adj.* 未吃晚饭的

therewith [ˌðeəˈwɪð] *adv.* 随后

The Partridge and the Fowler 斑鸠和捕鸟人

读一读，想一想

1. 斑鸠是怎样向捕鸟人求情的？
2. 捕鸟人为什么不放了斑鸠？

精彩故事欣赏

1 A fowler caught a partridge and was about to kill it. The partridge earnestly begged him to spare his life, saying, "Pray, master, permit me to live and I will entice many partridges to you in recompense for your mercy to me." The fowler replied, "I shall now with less scruple take your life, because you are willing to save it at the cost of betraying your friends and relations."

译 文

1 有个捕鸟人捉到一只斑鸠，要杀了它。斑鸠急切地哀求捕鸟人放了它："求求你放了我吧，我会吸引更多的斑鸠来献给你作为对你的报答。"捕鸟人却说道："听你这么一说，我杀你就更心安理得了，你竟然不惜陷害亲友的生命来换取自己的苟活。"

阅读无障碍

fowler [ˈfaʊlə] *n.* 捕野禽者
earnestly [ˈɜːnɪstlɪ] *adv.* 热切地
entice [ɪnˈtaɪs] *v.* 诱惑
in recompense for 以酬劳
mercy [ˈmɜːsi] *n.* 宽恕
scruple [ˈskruːpl] *n.* 良心上的不安
at the cost of 以……为代价
betray [bɪˈtreɪ] *v.* 出卖

The Fisherman and the Sprat

渔夫和小鲱鱼

读一读，想一想

1. 渔夫撒网收获了多少鱼？

2. 为什么渔夫不答应小鱼的哀求？

3. 从这个故事中可以学到什么？

精彩故事欣赏

1 A fisherman cast his net into the sea, and when he drew it up again it contained nothing but a single sprat that begged to be put back into the water. "I'm only a little fish now," it said, "but I shall grow big one day, and then if you come and catch me again I shall be of some use to you." But the fisherman replied, "Oh, no, I shall keep you now I've got you: if I put you back, should I ever see you again? Not likely!"

译　文

1 一个渔夫把网撒向大海，当他再次收网时，网里只有一只小鲱鱼，小鲱鱼苦苦哀求渔夫把它放回大海。"我现在只是一只小鱼，"它说，"但是我总有一天会长大，等到那时，你再来抓我，那时的我才会对你更有用。"然而，渔夫却回应道："不，不行，我现在就要抓住你，如果我放你回去，以后我还会再看到你吗？绝不可能了！"

阅读无障碍

cast [kɑːst] *v.* 抛

contain [kənˈteɪn] *v.* 包含

single [ˈsɪŋgl] *adj.* 惟一的

sprat [spræt] *n.* 小鲱鱼

The Fisherman Piping
吹笛子的渔夫

读一读，想一想

1. 渔夫为什么站在岩石上吹笛子？
2. 渔夫是怎样捕到鱼的？
3. 这个故事给我们什么启示？

1 A fisherman skilled in music took his flute and his nets to the seashore. Standing on a projecting rock, he played several tunes in the hope that the fish, attracted by his melody, would of their own accord dance into his net, which he had placed below. At last, having long waited in vain, he laid aside his flute, and casting his net into the sea, made an excellent haul of fish. When he saw them leaping about in the net upon the rock he said: "oh, you most perverse creatures, when I piped you would not dance, but now that I have

1 有个渔夫音乐上很有天赋，一天他带着笛子和渔网来到海边。渔夫站在一块突出的岩石上，吹起了笛子，希望鱼会被这美妙的音乐吸引纷纷主动跳到他已经张好的网里。然而过了好久，也没有一丁点收获。他只好放下笛子，拿起网撒向水里，结果捕到了许多鱼。看着在网里乱蹦乱跳的鱼，渔夫说："你们这些不识好歹

ceased you do so merrily."

的东西，我吹笛子时你们不跳舞，现在我不吹了，你们反而跳的这么欢！"

阅读无障碍

skilled [skɪld] *adj.* 有技能的
flute [fluːt] *n.* 笛子
projecting [prəˈdʒektɪŋ] *adj.* 突出的
several [ˈsevrəl] *adj.* 几个的
tune [tjuːn] *n.* 曲子
attract [əˈtrækt] *v.* 吸引
melody [ˈmelədi] *n.* 美妙的音乐
accord [əˈkɔːd] *n.* 一致
haul [hɔːl] *n.* 一网的捕获量
leap [liːp] *v.* 跳
perverse [pəˈvɜːs] *adj.* 故意作对的
pipe [paɪp] *v.* 用管乐器演奏
cease [siːs] *v.* 停止
merrily [ˈmerəli] *adv.* 快乐地

The Fisherman and His Nets

渔夫和他的网

读一读，想一想

1. 渔夫怎样防止大鱼跑掉?
2. 这个故事说明一个什么道理?

精彩故事欣赏

1 A fisherman, engaged in his calling, made a very successful cast and captured a great haul of fish. He managed by a skillful handling of his net to retain all the large fish and to draw them to the shore, but he could not prevent the smaller fish from falling back through the meshes of the net into the sea.

译 文

1 有个渔夫忙着打鱼，一网撒下去，打到很多鱼。他熟练地收网，然后拖到岸上，这样大鱼就不会跑掉了。但是却无法阻止小鱼从网眼里溜回大海。

阅读无障碍

engaged [ɪnˈgeɪdʒd] *adj.* 忙碌的

calling [ˈkɔːlɪŋ] *adj.* 职业

haul [hɔːl] *n.* 一网的捕获量

prevent [prɪˈvent] *v.* 阻止

mesh [meʃ] *n.* 网眼

The Charcoal-Burner and the Fuller

烧炭工和漂洗工

读一读，想一想

1. 烧炭工为什么邀请漂洗工同住？
2. 漂洗工为什么拒绝了烧炭工的邀请？
3. 这个故事的启示是什么？

1 A charcoal-burner carried on his trade in his own house. One day he met a friend, a fuller, and entreated him to come and live with him, saying that they should be far better neighbors and that their housekeeping expenses would be lessened. The fuller replied, "The arrangement is impossible as far as I am concerned, for whatever I should whiten, you would immediately blacken again with your charcoal."

1 一个烧炭人在自己房子里经营自己的买卖。一天他遇到一个做漂布生意的朋友，便邀请他搬来和他一起住，并解释说这样他们的关系会更亲密，两个人分担，家用也会减少。漂布人却回应说："这样的安排我不可能做到，因为无论我漂洗了什么，很快就会被你的炭弄黑。"

阅读无障碍

carry on 经营
entreat [ɪnˈtriːt] *v.* 请求
housekeeping [ˈhaʊskiːpɪŋ] *n.* 家用
expense [ɪkˈspens] *n.* 费用
lessen [ˈlesn] *v.* 减少
arrangement [əˈreɪndʒmənt] *n.* 安排
as far as I am concerned 就我而言
charcoal [ˈtʃɑːkəʊl] *n.* 木炭

The Spendthrift and the Swallow 败家子与燕子

1. 败家子为什么以为春天到了？
2. 早归的燕子最后结局是什么？
3. 通过这个故事我们明白一个什么道理？

精彩故事欣赏

1 A young man, a great spendthrift, had run through all his patrimony and had but one good cloak left. One day he happened to see a swallow, which had appeared before its season, skimming along a pool and twittering gaily. He supposed that spring had come, and went and sold his cloak. Not many days later, winter set in again with renewed frost and cold. When he found the unfortunate swallow lifeless on the ground, he said, "Unhappy bird! What have you done? By thus appearing before the springtime you have not only

译文

1 有个年轻的败家子，把家业都挥霍一空，只剩下一件不错的外衣。一天，他碰巧看到一只早归的燕子，一边叽叽喳喳地叫着一边掠过池塘。年轻人以为春天到了，就去把他仅有的那件外衣卖掉了。不料，没过几天，气温骤降，天寒地冻。败家子看到那只可怜的燕子掉在地上冻死了，他说："可怜的小鸟！看看你都做了什

killed yourself, but you have wrought my destruction also."

么！春天还没到你就提前出现，不仅害死了你自己，也把我害惨了。"

阅读无障碍

spendthrift [ˈspendθrɪft] *n.* 败家子

run through 挥霍

patrimony [ˈpætrɪməni] *n.* 祖传的财物

cloak [kləʊk] *n.* 外套

swallow [ˈswɒləʊ] *n.* 燕子

skimming [skɪm] *v.* 掠过

twittering [ˈtwɪtə(r)] *v.* 叽叽喳喳地叫

gaily [ˈgeɪli] *adv.* 快乐地

suppose [səˈpəʊz] *v.* 认为

renewed [rɪˈnjuːd] *adj.* 重新的

frost [frɒst] *n.* 严寒

unfortunate [ʌnˈfɔːtʃənət] *adj.* 不幸的

lifeless [ˈlaɪfləs] *adj.* 无生命的

wreak [riːk] *v.* 造成

destruction [dɪˈstrʌkʃn] *n.* 毁灭

The Old Woman and the Doctor 老太婆与医生

读一读，想一想

1. 老太婆和医生达成了什么协议？
2. 为什么老太婆拒绝按协议付钱？
3. 这个故事说明了一个怎样的做人道理？

精彩故事欣赏

1 An old woman having lost the use of her eyes, called in a physician to heal them, and made this bargain with him in the presence of witnesses: that if he should cure her blindness, he should receive from her a sum of money; but if her infirmity remained, she should give him nothing. This agreement being made, the physician, time after time, applied his salve to her eyes, and on every visit took something away, stealing all her property little by little. And when he had got all she had, he healed her and demanded the

译 文

1 有位老太婆患了眼疾失明了，就请一位医生给她治病，在见证人的帮助下达成了治疗协议：如果医生能治好她的眼疾，就会得到丰厚的报酬；但是如果治不好，他一分也得不到。于是医生按照协议定期一次次来她家进行治疗，并且每次都趁老太婆闭着眼睛的时候，顺手牵羊地一点一点地偷走所有东西。当他把老太

promised payment. The old woman, when she recovered her sight and saw none of her goods in her house, would give him nothing. The physician insisted on his claim, and as she still refused, summoned her before the judge. The old woman, standing up in the court, argued: "This man here speaks the truth in what he says: for I did promise to give him a sum of money if I should recover my sight, but if I continued blind, I was to give him nothing. Now he declares that I am healed. I on the contrary affirm that I am still blind: for when I lost the use of my eyes, I saw in my house various chattels and valuable goods, but now, though he swears I am cured of my blindness, I am not able to see a single thing in it."

婆家里的东西都偷光了的时候，老太婆的眼睛也终于治好了。医生便向老太婆索要商定好的报酬，老太婆睁开眼睛发现家里空荡荡的，就拒绝付钱。医生几次三番坚持索要报酬，但老太婆就是不给。于是把她带到法官那里。站在法庭上，老太婆申辩道："这个人说的是事实，我的确许诺过如果他治好了我的眼疾，我就付给他大笔钱。现在他声称我已经康复了，可是相反，我仍然失明并且，以前我还能看见家里的各种财产物品，可是现在他说治好了我，而我却什么东西都看不到了。"

阅读无障碍

physician [fɪˈzɪʃn] *n.* 医生
heal [hiːl] *v.* 治疗
witness [ˈwɪtnəs] *n.* 见证人
a sum of 一笔
infirmity [ɪnˈfɜːməti] *n.* 病症
apply to 致力于
payment [ˈpeɪmənt] *n.* 报酬

insist [ɪnˈsɪst] *v.* 坚持
summon [ˈsʌmən] *v.* 传唤
declare [dɪˈkleə(r)] *v.* 声称
on the contrary 正相反
various [ˈveəriəs] *adj.* 各种各样的
chattel [ˈtʃætl] *n.* 财产
valuable [ˈvæljuəbl] *adj.* 贵重的

The Boys and the Frogs
男孩和青蛙

读一读，想一想

1. 男孩们在池塘边干什么？
2. 为什么青蛙请求男孩不要扔石头？
3. 老青蛙的话给我们什么启示？

精彩故事欣赏

1 One spring day some naughty boys were playing near a pond. They began to throw stones into the water. In the pond lived many frogs were much afraid of the boys, for the stones hurt some of the frogs. At last an old frog lifted his head out of the water and said, "Boys, please don't throw stones at us."

2 The boys said, "We are only playing." "I know that, but please stop throwing stones, my boys. What is play to you is death to us," said the old frog.

3 So the boys stopped throwing stones and went away.

译文

1 春天里的一天，一些淘气的男孩在一个池塘边玩耍。他们开始往水里扔石头。池塘里面住着许多青蛙，他们非常害怕这些男孩，因为一些青蛙曾被石头打伤过。最后一只老青蛙把他的脑袋探出水面，说道："孩子们，请你们别再朝我们扔石头了。"

2 男孩说："我们只是在玩。""我知道，但请不要扔石头，孩子们。对你们来说只是玩耍，可对我们来说却意味着死亡。”老青蛙说道。

3 于是男孩们不再扔石头，离开了池塘。

naughty [ˈnɔːti] *adj.* 淘气的

pond [pɒnd] *n.* 池塘

be afraid of 害怕

lift [lɪft] *v.* 抬起

The Mistress and Her Servants 女主人和仆人

读一读，想一想

1. 侍女们为什么痛恨那只公鸡？
2. 公鸡被弄死后，侍女们得偿所愿了吗？
3. 这个故事说明了什么？

1 A widow, thrifty and industrious, had two servants, whom she kept pretty hard at work. They were not allowed to lie long abed in the mornings, but the old lady had them up and doing as soon as the cockerel crew. They disliked intensely having to get up at such an hour, especially in winter-time, and they thought that if it were not for the cockerel waking up their mistress so horribly early, they could sleep longer. So they caught it and wrung its neck. But they weren't prepared for the consequences. For what happened was that

1 有个勤劳节俭的寡妇，雇了两个侍女，每日让她们干很多活。她们不能睡懒觉，夜里每当公鸡一打鸣，她就叫她们起来去干活。侍女们非常痛恨那么早就起来干活，尤其是寒冬时分。她们想，要不是因为那只公鸡不到天亮就叫醒女主人的话，她们肯定还能多睡会。所以她们抓住那只公鸡拧断了它的脖子。然而结果是他们没

their mistress, not hearing the cockerel crow as usual, waked them up earlier than ever, and set them to work in the middle of the night.

想到女主人会听不到鸡鸣声，总是更早地把她们叫起来，在半夜里去干活。

阅读无障碍

widow [ˈwɪdəʊ] *n.* 寡妇
thrifty [ˈθrɪfti] *adj.* 节俭的
industrious [ɪnˈdʌstriəs] *adj.* 勤劳的
servant [ˈsɜːvənt] *n.* 仆人
abed [əˈbed] *adv.* 在床上
cockerel [ˈkɒkərəl] *n.* 小公鸡
crow [krəʊ] *v.* 鸡啼报晓
intensely [ɪnˈtenslɪ] *adv.* 强烈地
especially [ɪˈspeʃəli] *adv.* 尤其地
horribly [ˈhɒrəblɪ] *adv.* 非常地
wrung [rɪŋ] *v.* 拧
consequence [ˈkɒnsɪkwəns] *n.* 结果

The Milkmaid and Her Pail
挤奶女孩和她的桶

读一读，想一想

1. 女孩去集市的时候边走边干什么？
2. 为什么牛奶洒出来了？
3. 女孩的结局告诉我们什么？

精彩故事欣赏

1 A milkmaid was going to the market. She carried her milk in a pail on her head. As she went along she began calculating what she would buy after she had sold the milk. "I'll buy a new dress, and when I go to the ball, all the young men will dance with me!" As she spoke she tossed her head and all the milk was spilt.The girl went back without anything. She felt very sad. "Ah, my child," said her mother. "Do not count your chickens before they are hatched."

译　文

1 一个农家挤奶姑娘头上顶着一桶牛奶，往集市走去。她一边走一边开始计算卖完牛奶后要买的东西:"我要买一件新裙子，等我参加舞会的时候，年轻的小伙子都会邀请我跳舞。"想到这里，她轻轻晃起头来，结果头上的牛奶桶摔在地上，牛奶都洒出来了。女孩手空空地回到家里，感到非常伤心。"我的孩子，"母亲对她说，"不要过早地打如意算盘。"

阅读无障碍

milkmaid [ˈmɪlkmeɪd] *n.* 挤奶女工

pail [peɪl] *n.* 桶

calculate [ˈkælkjuleɪt] *v.* 计算

ball [bɔːl] *n.* 舞会

toss [tɒs] *v.* 摇

spill [spɪl] *v.* 洒出

hatch [hætʃ] *v.* 孵出

The Bear and the Travellers
熊和旅人

1. 遇到熊以后，两个旅行者是怎么做的？
2. 为什么熊放过了躺在地上的旅行者？
3. 真正的朋友应该是什么样的朋友？

精彩故事欣赏

1 Two travellers were on the road together, when a bear suddenly appeared on the scene. Before he observed them, one made for a tree at the side of the road, and climbed up into the branches and hid there. The other was not so nimble as his companion, and, as he could not escape, he threw himself on the ground and pretended to be dead. The bear came up and sniffed all round him, but he kept perfectly still and held his breath: for they say that a bear will not touch a dead body. The bear took him for a corpse, and went away.

1 两个旅行者一起出行，突然前面出现了一头熊。还没等熊看到他们，其中一个立刻冲向路边爬到树上藏了起来。另一个人不如他的同伴那样敏捷，眼见自己逃不掉了，就直挺挺地躺在地上装起死来。熊走到他跟前，在他周围嗅了嗅，这个人一直屏住呼吸，安然不动，因为他听说熊是不吃死人的。熊果然把他当成了死

When the coast was clear, the Traveller in the tree came down, and asked the other what it was the bear had whispered to him when he put his mouth to his ear. The other replied, "He told me never again to travel with a friend who deserts you at the first sign of danger."

尸，然后走开了。当危险解除以后，另一个旅行者从树上下来，问那个人当他躺在地上装死时，熊在他耳边说了什么。那人答道，"他告诉我以后再也不要和一个遇到危险就丢下朋友不管的人做朋友了。"

阅读无障碍

suddenly [ˈsʌdənli] *adv.* 忽然地
observe [əbˈzɜːv] *v.* 注意
nimble [ˈnɪmbl] *adj.* 敏捷的
companion [kəmˈpæniən] *n.* 同伴
pretend [prɪˈtend] *v.* 假装
sniff [snɪf] *v.* 嗅
perfectly [ˈpɜːfɪktli] *adv.* 完全地
corpse [kɔːps] *n.* 死尸
the coast is clear 危险已过
desert [ˈdezət] *v.* 抛弃
at the first sign of 当有……迹象时

The Slave and the Lion
奴隶和狮子

读一读，想一想

1. 狮子为什么不吃了奴隶？
2. 奴隶主是怎样惩罚奴隶的？
3. 最终的结果给我们什么启示？

精彩故事欣赏

1 A slave ran away from his master, by whom he had been most cruelly treated, and, in order to avoid capture, betook himself into the desert. As he wandered about in search of food and shelter, he came to a cave, which he entered and found to be unoccupied. Really, however, it was a lion's den, and almost immediately, to the horror of the wretched fugitive, the lion himself appeared. The man gave himself up for lost, but, to his utter astonishment, the lion, instead of springing upon him and devouring him, came and

译 文

1 一个奴隶不堪忍受主人的虐待逃跑了。为了避免被抓住，他逃进沙漠中。正当他到处游荡寻找食物和栖身地时，他来到了一个洞穴。他走进洞穴发现里面空无一人，然而，这实际上是一个狮子的巢穴。突然一只狮子出现了，这个可怜的逃亡者吓坏了。他万念俱灰，但是出人意料的是，狮子不但没有扑过来吃掉他，反而可怜

fawned upon him, at the same time whining and lifting up his paw. Observing it to be much swollen and inflamed, he examined it and found a large thorn embedded in the ball of the foot. He accordingly removed it and dressed the wound as well as he could, and in course of time it healed up completely. The lion's gratitude was unbounded, he looked upon the man as his friend, and they shared the cave for some time together. A day came, however, when the slave began to long for the society of his fellow-men, and he bade farewell to the lion and returned to the town. Here he was presently recognized and carried off in chains to his former master, who resolved to make an example of him, and ordered that he should be thrown to the beasts at the next public spectacle in the theatre. On the fatal day the beasts were loosed into the arena, and among the rest a lion of huge bulk and ferocious aspect, and then the wretched slave was cast in among them. What was the amazement of the spectators, when the lion after one glance bounded up to him and lay down at his feet with every expression of affection and delight! It was his old friend of the cave! The audience clamored that the slave's life should be spared, and the governor of the town, marveling at such gratitude and fidelity in a beast, decreed that both should receive their liberty.

巴巴地来到他面前，一边哀嚎，一边把爪子伸出来。奴隶看到狮爪红肿发炎，就仔细检查了一下，发现有一根大刺深深地扎在里面。于是他把刺拔了出来并尽可能地处理好了伤口。渐渐地，伤口痊愈了。狮子对他感激不尽，把他当成了自己的朋友，之后的一段时间他们一起住在这个洞穴里。终于有一天，奴隶开始渴望回到人类社会，于是他告别狮子，回到镇子上。他刚一露面，马上就被认出来，很快就被抓起来带上镣铐，送到以前的主人那里。为了以儆效尤，主人命令把他送到竞技场，在下次表演时把他扔给野兽。到了生死攸关的这天，野兽都被放进竞技场，其中有一头体态肥大、面貌凶恶的狮子，接着奴隶也被扔了进去。令所有观众惊讶的是，狮子一看见这个奴隶，立刻兴奋地跑到他跟前，趴在他脚边。这正是曾经和他一起在洞中生活过的老朋友！观众们大声喊着应该饶了这个奴隶，镇上的官员对这只野兽的感恩与忠诚感到惊讶，于是下令让奴隶和狮子都重获自由。

阅读无障碍

cruelly [ˈkruːəlɪ] *adv.* 残酷地
capture [ˈkæptʃə(r)] *n.* 捕获
betook [bɪˈtʊk] *v.* 去
wander about 四处游荡
in search of 寻找
unoccupied [ˌʌnˈɑkjupaɪd] *adj.* 空闲的；没人住的
den [den] *n.* 兽穴
horror [ˈhɒrə(r)] *n.* 恐怖
wretched [ˈretʃɪd] *adj.* 可怜的
fugitive [ˈfjuːdʒətɪv] *n.* 逃命者
astonishment [əˈstɒnɪʃmənt] *n.* 惊讶
spring [sprɪŋ] *v.* 跳
devour [dɪˈvaʊə(r)] *v.* 吞没
fawn [fɔːn] *v.* 摇尾乞怜
swollen [ˈswəʊlən] *adj.* 肿起的
inflamed [ɪnˈfleɪmd] *adj.* 发炎的
embedded [ɪmˈbedɪd] *adj.* 深入的
accordingly [əˈkɔːdɪŋli] *adv.* 于是
in course of time 终于
heal up 愈合
unbounded [ʌnˈbaʊndɪd] *adj.* 无限的
long for 思念
society [səˈsaɪəti] *n.* 社会
bid farewell to 告别
recognize [ˈrekəgnaɪz] *v.* 认出
spectacle [ˈspektəkl] *n.* 表演
arena [əˈriːnə] *n.* 竞技场
ferocious [fəˈrəʊʃəs] *adj.* 残忍的
amazement [əˈmeɪzmənt] *n.* 惊奇
audience [ˈɔːdiəns] *n.* 观众
clamor [ˈklæmə] *v.* 大声地要求或抗议
governor [ˈgʌvənə(r)] *n.* 统治者
marvel [ˈmɑːvl] *v.* 对……感到惊奇
fidelity [fɪˈdeləti] *n.* 忠诚

The Flea and the Man

跳蚤和人

读一读，想一想

1. 这个人为什么恼火？
2. 跳蚤是怎样为自己求情的？
3. 故事的结局说明了什么？

精彩故事欣赏

1 A man, very much annoyed with a flea, caught him at last, and said, "Who are you who dare to feed on my limbs, and to cost me so much trouble in catching you?" The flea replied, "Oh my dear sir, pray spare my life, and destroy me not, for I cannot possibly do you much harm." The man, laughing, replied, "Now you shall certainly die by My? own hands, for no evil, whether it be small or large, ought to be tolerated."

译 文

1 有个人被一只跳蚤弄得心烦意乱，十分恼火。最后这个人捉住了跳蚤，问它："你算是什么东西呀，胆敢在我身上到处咬，费了我九牛二虎之力才捉到你？"跳蚤回答说："亲爱的先生，请饶了我吧，千万别捏死我，我不可能给你造成多大的伤害。"那人大笑道："罪恶不论大小，都不应饶恕，所以我一定要捏死你。"

阅读无障碍

annoyed [əˈnɔɪd] *adj.* 恼怒的
flea [fliː] *n.* 跳蚤
limb [lɪm] *n.* 四肢
destroy [dɪˈstrɔɪ] *v.* 杀死
tolerated [ˈtɒləreɪt] *v.* 容忍

The Blind Man and the Cub
盲人与小野兽

读一读，想一想

1. 瞎子擅长什么？
2. 瞎子的话跟我们什么启示？
3. 有句话叫“三岁看老”是什么意思？

精彩故事欣赏

1 A blind man was accustomed to distinguishing different animals by touching them with his hands. The whelp of a wolf was brought him, with a request that he would feel it, and say what it was. He felt it, and being in doubt, said: “I do not quite know whether it is the cub of a fox, or the whelp of a wolf, but this I know full well: It would not be safe to admit him to the sheepfold.”

译 文

1 一个瞎子精于用手触摸辨别各种动物。一天有人把一头小狼带到他面前，请他摸一摸，说出是什么东西。他摸了摸这个小野兽后，有点不确定，说道：“我不能肯定这是一只小狐狸，还是一头小狼，但是有一点我却能十分肯定，如果让它进羊圈的话将会很危险。”

阅读无障碍

be accustomed to 习惯于
distinguish [dɪˈstɪŋgwɪʃ] *v.* 辨别
doubt [daʊt] *n.* 怀疑
full [fʊl] *adv.* 极其地

The Boy and the Snails

男孩和蜗牛

读一读，想一想

1. 男孩抓了蜗牛后做了什么？
2. 蜗牛感到热了以后是怎么做的？
3. 这个故事说明一个什么道理？

精彩故事欣赏

1 A farmer's boy went looking for snails, and, when he had picked up both his hands full, he set about making a fire at which to roast them, for he meant to eat them. When it got well alight and the snails began to feel the heat, they gradually withdrew more and more into their shells with the hissing noise they always make when they do so. When the boy heard it, he said, "You abandoned creatures, how can you find heart to whistle when your houses are burning?"

译文

1 一个乡下男孩到处寻找蜗牛，当他双手抓满了蜗牛后，他想吃它们，于是开始准备生火烤这些蜗牛。火点着后慢慢烧旺了，蜗牛也开始感觉到热了，于是他们像往常一样渐渐缩进壳里，还发出吱吱的声音。男孩子听到了吱吱声后说道："你们这些连命都快没有的家伙，壳都要被烧掉了怎么还能有心情吹口哨呢？"

snail [sneɪl] *n.* 蜗牛

set about 开始做

roast [rəʊst] *v.* 烤

alight [əˈlaɪt] *adj.* 烧着的

gradually [ˈɡrædʒuəli] *adv.* 逐渐地

withdrew [wɪðˈdruː] *v.* 撤回

hissing [hɪsɪŋ] *adj.* 发出滋滋声的

abandoned [əˈbændənd] *adj.* 被遗弃的

creature [ˈkriːtʃə(r)] *n.* 生物

whistle [ˈwɪsl] *v.* 吹口哨

The Apes and the Two Travellers 猿猴和两个旅人

读一读，想一想

1. 骑手是怎样得到兔子的？
2. 猎人追上骑手了吗？
3. 猎人是一个真正慷慨的人吗？为什么？

精彩故事欣赏

1 Two men, one who always spoke the truth and the other who told nothing but lies, were traveling together and by chance came to the land of apes. One of the apes, who had raised himself to be king, commanded them to be seized and brought before him, that he might know what was said of him among men. He ordered at the same time that all the apes be arranged in a long row on his right hand and on his left, and that a throne be placed for him, as was the custom among men. After these preparations he signified that the two men should be brought before him, and greeted

译 文

1 有两个人，一个总是说实话，另一个专门说假话，一起去旅行。偶然来到了猿猴国。猴王吩咐手下把他们捉拿住，带到它面前，这样它有可能就会知道人类是怎么评价它的。同时它命令所有的猿猴在它左右排成两行，并且按照人类的习惯给它放上宝座。一切准备好了以后，它下令把那两个人带过来，开始招呼他们：“陌生人，你们觉得我是一个什

them with this salutation: "What sort of a king do I seem to you to be, O strangers?" The lying traveler replied, "You seem to me a most mighty king." "And what is your estimate of those you see around me?" "These," he made answer, "are worthy companions of yourself, fit at least to be ambassadors and leaders of armies." The ape and all his court, gratified with the lie, commanded that a handsome present be given to the flatterer. On this the truthful traveler thought to himself, "If so great a reward be given for a lie, with what gift may not I be rewarded, if, according to my custom, I tell the truth?" The ape quickly turned to him. "And pray how do I and these my friends around me seem to you?" "Thou art," he said, "a most excellent ape, and all these thy companions after thy example are excellent apes too." The king of the apes, enraged at hearing these truths, gave him over to the teeth and claws of his companions.

么样的国王呢？”专说假话的旅行者回答说：“在我看来你是世界上最强大的国王。”猴王又问道：“那你认为我周围的手下怎么样？”“他们，”他回答说，“是出色的臣民，至少都可以当大使和将军。”听了他的假话猴王和他的手下都非常满意，吩咐给这位马屁精一件好礼物。看到这种情况那个诚实的旅行者心想：“一句谎言都能得到如此重赏，那如果我还是按照习惯说实话的话，又怎么会得不到奖赏呢？”猴王很快朝着他问道：“请告诉我你认为我和我周围的手下怎样？”他说：“你相当棒，如果所有的猿猴都学你的样子的话也会非常出色。”听到这些实话，猴王暴怒，命令手下用牙齿和爪子去收拾他。

阅读无障碍

by chance 偶然地
ape [eɪp] *n.* 猿猴
arrange [əˈreɪndʒ] *v.* 安排
throne [θrəʊn] *n.* 宝座
custom [ˈkʌstəm] *n.* 习惯
signify [ˈsɪgnɪfaɪ] *v.* 表示
salutation [ˌsæljuˈteɪʃn] *n.* 招呼
mighty [ˈmaɪti] *adj.* 强大的
estimate [ˈestɪmət] *n.* 评价
ambassador [æmˈbæsədə(r)] *n.* 大使
gratify [ˈgrætɪfaɪ] *v.* 满意
flatterer [ˈflætərə(r)] *n.* 奉承者
truthful [ˈtruːθfl] *adj.* 诚实的
enrage [ɪnˈreɪdʒ] *v.* 暴怒

The Shepherd's Boy and the Wolf 牧童和狼

1. 为什么一开始邻居们来帮放羊娃？
2. 后来狼来了，为什么村民们反而不来帮忙了？
3. 从这个故事中我们能学到什么？

精彩故事欣赏

1 A shepherd boy was watching a flock of sheep near his village. He felt very bored. He cried out to the village: "Wolf! Wolf!" though there was no wolf at all. When his neighbors came to help him, he laughed at them for their pains. He repeated this trick four times and his neighbors were cheated four times. The wolf however did truly come at last. The shepherd boy shouted in a pain of terror: "Wolf! Wolf! Do come and help me, the wolf is killing the sheep," but no one paid any attention to his cries, nor did anyone

1 一个牧童正在村子附近放羊。他感到太无聊了，想找点乐子。于是对着村子大喊："狼来了！狼来了！"实际上根本没有狼来。当他的邻居们跑来帮忙时，却遭到了他的嘲笑。他将这个恶作剧玩了四次，而他的邻居们也被他骗了四次。后来有一天狼真地来了，牧童恐怖万分，大声呼救："狼真的来了！狼真来了！大家快来

give him any assistance. The wolf had no cause of fear and took it easily, and finally destroyed the whole flock.

帮忙啊！狼在吃羊啊！”但是，没有人再去注意他的呼救，更没有人来帮忙。狼于是肆无忌惮，轻松地吃着羊，最后，把整个羊群都吃掉了。

pain [peɪn] *n.* 作为辛劳的回报
repeat [rɪˈpiːt] *v.* 重复
trick [trɪk] *n.* 恶作剧
cheat [tʃiːt] *v.* 欺骗
terror [ˈterə(r)] *n.* 恐惧
attention [əˈtenʃn] *n.* 注意
assistance [əˈsɪstəns] *n.* 帮助
cause [kɔːz] *n.* 理由
flock [flɒk] *n.* 羊群

The Boasting Traveller

吹牛的旅人

读一读，想一想

1. 这个人回国后对别人吹嘘什么？
2. 大家相信他吗？
3. 这个故事告诉我们什么？

1 A man once went abroad on his travels, and when he came home he had wonderful tales to tell of the things he had done in foreign countries. Among other things, he said he had taken part in a jumping-match at Rhodes, and had done a wonderful jump which no one could beat. "Just go to Rhodes and ask them," he said; "every one will tell you it's true." But one of those who were listening said, "If you can jump as well as all that, we needn't go to Rhodes to prove it. Let's just imagine this is Rhodes for a minute: and now -- jump!"

1 一次有个人从国外旅行回来，对他在外国的精彩经历大肆吹嘘。比如他说自己在罗德岛参加了跳远比赛，他跳的最远，无人能敌。“不信的话可以去罗德岛找人问问，”他说，“当时在场的每个人都能证明。”这时旁边一个听众说：“如果你真的跳得那么好的话，根本不需要去罗德岛找人证明。你就把这里当成罗德岛，现在再跳一次吧？”

abroad [əˈbrɔːd] *adv.* 到国外

tale [teɪl] *n.* 故事

foreign [ˈfɒrən] *adj.* 外国的

beat [biːt] *v.* 打败

imagine [ɪˈmædʒɪn] *v.* 想像

The Huntsman and the Fisherman 猎人和渔夫

1. 猎人和渔夫为什么交换自己的收获？
2. 邻居认为如果他们继续交换会出现什么情况？
3. 这个寓言说明了什么？

精彩故事欣赏

1 A huntsman, returning with his dogs from the field, fell in by chance with a fisherman who was bringing home a basket well laden with fish. The huntsman wished to have the fish, and their owner experienced an equal longing for the contents of the game-bag. They quickly agreed to exchange the produce of their day's sport. Each was so well pleased with his bargain that they made for sometime the same exchange day after day. Finally a neighbor said to them, "If you go on in this way, you will soon destroy by frequent use

1 一个猎人带着猎狗从野外打猎回来，路上碰巧遇到一个带着沉甸甸的鱼篓满载而归的渔夫。猎人非常想要渔夫的鱼，而渔夫正好也眼馋猎人狩猎袋中的猎物。于是两人很快就互换了一天的收获。两人都很满意从对方那里交换得来的东西，于是一段时间每天都交换所得。最后，一个邻居对他们说："如果你们继续这样交换

the pleasure of your exchange, and each will again wish to retain the fruits of his own sport."

的话，很快就会失去交换的乐趣，到时候你们就又希望得到自己的劳动成果了。"

fall in with 碰见
laden [ˈleɪdn] *adj.* 满载的
content [ˈkɒntent] *n.* 内容
game-bag [ˈgeɪmbˈæg] *n.* 狩猎袋
frequent [ˈfriːkwənt] *adj.* 频繁的
retain [rɪˈteɪn] *v.* 保留

The Dog and the Cook

狗和厨师

读一读，想一想

1. 这只可怜的狗为什么去了宴会？
2. 它是怎样从离开宴会的？
3. 这个故事说明了什么？

精彩故事欣赏

1 A rich man gave a great feast, to which he invited many friends and acquaintances. His dog availed himself of the occasion to invite a stranger dog, a friend of his, saying, "My master gives a feast, and there is always much food remaining, come and sup with me tonight." The dog thus invited went at the hour appointed, and seeing the preparations for so grand an entertainment, said in the joy of his heart, "How glad I am that I came! I do not often get such a chance as this. I will take care and eat enough to last me

译　文

1 一位富人要开一个盛大的宴会，他请了许多朋友和熟人。他的狗趁机邀请了自己的伙伴另一只狗来参加宴会，他说："我的主人设摆筵席，总是会剩下许多食物，今晚你来和我一起吃。"那只狗因此接受了邀请，及时到了宴会地点。看到如此盛大的准备，它心花怒放，说道："我能来这儿太高兴了！这样的机会可不常有。

both today and tomorrow." While he was congratulating himself and wagging his tail to convey his pleasure to his friend, the cook saw him moving about among his dishes and seizing him by his fore and hind paws, bundled him without ceremony out of the window. He fell with force upon the ground and limped away, howling dreadfully. His yelling soon attracted other street dogs, who came up to him and inquired how he had enjoyed his supper. He replied, "Why, to tell you the truth, I drank so much wine that I remember nothing. I do not know how I got out of the house."

我一定会照顾好自己，吃够今天和明天的。”当它暗自庆幸，摇着尾巴向朋友表达它的愉悦之情时，厨师看见了它在盘子周围转悠，于是抓住他的前爪和后爪，毫不客气地把它从窗户扔了出去。它一下子摔在地上，爬起来一瘸一拐地哀嚎着离开了。它的嚎叫声很快吸引了其他街头流浪狗。它们过来问它是怎样享用晚餐的。它回答说：“啥？说实话，我喝了太多酒，记不清了。我不知道我是怎样走出房子的。”

阅读无障碍

acquaintance [əˈkweɪntəns] *n.* 熟人
avail [əˈveɪl] *v.* 利用（机会）
occasion [əˈkeɪʒn] *n.* 时机
sup [sʌp] *v.* 吃晚饭
preparation [ˌprepəˈreɪʃn] *n.* 准备
entertainment [ˌentəˈteɪnmənt] *n.* 招待
congratulate [kənˈgrætʃuleɪt] *v.* 为（自己）感到高兴
wag [wæg] *v.* 摇动
convey [kənˈveɪ] *v.* 表达
seize [siːz] *v.* 抓住
bundle [ˈbʌndl] *v.* 匆忙打发
ceremony [ˈserəməni] *n.* 客气
howling [haʊl] *v.* 哀嚎
dreadfully [ˈdredfəli] *adv.* 非常沮丧的
yelling [jelɪŋ] *v.* 嚎叫
inquire [ɪnˈkwaɪə(r)] *v.* 询问

The Thieves and the Cock

小偷和公鸡

读一读，想一想

1. 小偷们在这户人家偷了什么？
2. 小偷们会放了公鸡吗？为什么？
3. 这个故事说明了什么道理？

精彩故事欣赏

1 Some thieves broke into a house and found nothing but a cock, whom they stole, and got off as fast as they could. Upon arriving at home they prepared to kill the cock, who thus pleaded for his life: "Pray spare me; I am very serviceable to men. I wake them up in the night to their work." "That is the very reason why we must the more kill you," they replied, "for when you wake your neighbors, you entirely put an end to our business."

译 文

1 几个小偷悄悄地溜进一户人家里，什么也没偷到，只找到一只公鸡，于是偷了公鸡迅速溜走了。当小偷们回到家准备杀公鸡时，公鸡哀求小偷们放了他："请饶我一命，我对人们很有用。每天天不亮时，我就把人们叫起来工作。""单凭这一点，我们就必须杀了你，"小偷们说道，"你把人们都叫醒了，我们就偷不成东西了。"

break into 闯入

prepare [prɪˈpeə(r)] *v.* 准备

plead [pliːd] *v.* 恳求

spare [speə(r)] *n.* 饶命

serviceable [ˈsɜːvɪsəbl] *adj.* 有用的

entirely [ɪnˈtaɪəli] *adv.* 完全地

The Farmer and Fortune
农夫和命运之神

读一读，想一想

1. 农夫犁地时发现了什么？
2. 命运之神为什么责备农夫？
3. 农夫是个怎样的人？

精彩故事欣赏

1 A Farmer was ploughing one day on his farm when he turned up a pot of golden coins with his plough. He was overjoyed at his discovery, and from that time forth made an offering daily at the shrine of the Goddess of the Earth. Fortune was displeased at this, and came to him and said, "My man, why do you give Earth the credit for the gift which I bestowed upon you? You never thought of thanking me for your good luck, but should you be unlucky enough to lose what you have gained I know very well that I, Fortune, should then come in for all the blame."

译　文

1 有个农夫用犁耕地时耙出一坛子金币，他对自己的发现欣喜若狂。从那之后，他每天都用供品来供奉土地爷。命运之神对此很生气，来到他面前对他说："你这个人怎么回事，那坛金币明明是我送给你的礼物，你为什么却供奉土地爷呢？得到好运时你从未想到要感谢我，但是如果你不幸丢了东西时，我敢肯定，你一定会埋怨我。"

plough [ˈplaʊ] v. 用犁耕田
turn up 翻起
bestow [bɪˈstəʊ] v. 赠给

Father and Sons

父亲和儿子

读一读，想一想

1. 父亲为什么感到烦恼？
2. 父亲最后用了什么方法来教育他的儿子们？
3. 这个故事说明了什么道理？

精彩故事欣赏

1 A father had a family of sons who were perpetually quarreling among themselves. When he failed to heal their disputes by his exhortations, he determined to give them a practical illustration of the evils of disunion, and for this purpose he one day told them to bring him a bundle of sticks. When they had done so, he placed the faggot into the hands of each of them in succession, and ordered them to break it in pieces. They tried with all their strength, and were not able to do it. He next opened the faggot, took the sticks separately, one

译　文

1 有个父亲家有好几个儿子。这几个儿子整天吵个不停。他多次劝解都无济于事，最后他决定用实际的例子来教育儿子们。一天，他让儿子们去拿一捆柴来。当他们把木柴拿来后，他便依次地将那捆柴放在每一个孩子的手中，让他们把这捆柴折断。儿子们用尽全力也无法将它折断。随后他解开了那捆木棒，给他们每人一

by one, and again put them into his sons' hands, upon which they broke them easily. He then addressed them in these words: "My sons, if you are of one mind, and unite to assist each other, you will be as this faggot, uninjured by all the attempts of your enemies; but if you are divided among yourselves, you will be broken as easily as these sticks."

根，让他们再试。这下他们毫不费力地就折断了。这时，父亲语重心长地说："孩子们，如果你们团结一致，齐心协力，就会像这捆木柴一样，不能被你们的敌人打垮；可如果你们各自为营，斗个不停，你们就会像这些散柴一样不堪一击。"

阅读无障碍

family [ˈfæmɪlɪ] *n.* 子女
perpetually [pəˈpetʃʊəlɪ] *adv.* 持久地
quarrel [ˈkwɒrəl] *v.* 吵架
heal [hiːl] *v.* 和解
dispute [dɪˈspjuːt] *n.* 争吵
exhortation [egzɔːˈteɪʃən] *n.* 劝告
determine [dɪˈtɜːmɪn] *v.* 决定
illustration [ɪləˈstreɪʃən] *n.* 例证
evil [ˈiːvl] *n.* 不幸
disunion [dɪsˈjuːnjən] *n.* 分裂；不统一
bundle [ˈbʌndl] *n.* 捆
faggot [ˈfægət] *n.* 柴把
succession [səkˈseʃən] *n.* 连续
separately [ˈseprətlɪ] *adv.* 分离地
address [əˈdres] *v.* 对……说话
unite [juːˈnaɪt] *v.* 团结
assist [əˈsɪst] *v.* 帮助
uninjured [ʌnˈɪndʒəd] *adj.* 未受伤害的

The Boy Bathing
洗澡的小男孩

读一读，想一想

1. 小男孩向路人求救，路人是怎么做的？
2. 遇到问题后只会责备有用吗？

精彩故事欣赏

1 A boy bathing in a river was in danger of being drowned. He called out to a passing traveler for help, but instead of holding out a helping hand, the man stood by unconcernedly, and scolded the boy for his imprudence. "Oh, sir!" cried the youth, "pray help me now and scold me afterwards."

译文

1 有个小男孩在河里洗澡，遇到了危险，眼看要被淹死了。正巧有人路过，男孩大声呼救。然而，那人不但没有救起小男孩，反而漠不关心地站在旁边责备小男孩太冒险。"哦，先生，"小男孩喊道："请你还是先把我救起来后再责备我吧。"

阅读无障碍

drown [draʊn] *v.* 淹死
hold out 伸出
unconcernedly [ˌʌnkənˈsɜːnɪdlɪ] *adv.* 漠不关心地
scold [skəʊld] *v.* 责备
imprudence [ɪmˈpruːdns] *n.* 轻率行为
afterwards [ˈɑːftəwədz] *adv.* 然后

The Boy and the Nettles

男孩和荨麻

读一读，想一想

1. 小男孩在地里玩的时候发生了什么事？
2. 为什么小男孩会被荨麻扎伤手？
3. 这个故事说明了什么道理？

精彩故事欣赏

1 A boy was playing in the fields when he was stung by a nettle. He ran home to tell his mother what had happened.

2 "I only touched it lightly," he said, "and the nasty thing stung me."

3 "It stung you because you only touched it lightly," his mother told him, "Next time you touch a nettle grasp it as tightly as you can. Then it won't sting you at all."

译　文

1 一个男孩子在地里玩，突然被荨麻刺伤了。他跑回家去，告诉妈妈发生了什么事。

2 "我只是轻轻地碰了它一下，"他说，"那讨厌的东西就扎到我了。"

3 "正因为你只轻轻地碰它，它才扎到你，"妈妈对他说，"下次你再碰到荨麻，就紧紧地抓住它。那它反而就根本不会扎到你了。"

nettle ['netl] *n.* 荨麻

lightly ['laɪtli] *adv.* 轻轻地

nasty ['nɑ:sti] *adj.* 令人讨厌的

grasp [grɑ:sp] *v.* 抓住

The Peasant and the Apple-tree 农夫和苹果树

读一读，想一想

1. 最初农夫为什么要砍掉苹果树？
2. 农夫最终砍掉苹果树了吗？为什么？

精彩故事欣赏

1 A peasant had an apple-tree growing in his garden, which bore no fruit, but could only provide a shelter for the sparrows and cicadas which sat and chirped in its branches. Disappointed at its barrenness, he decided to cut it down. Sparrows and the cicadas saw what the peasant was about to do, they begged him to spare the tree, "If you destroy the tree, we shall have to seek another shelter, and you will no longer have our chirping to enliven your work" He ,however, refused to listen to them, and set to work with an axe. After a few blows, he reached the hollow of the tree and found a hive full of honey. Delighted with his

译 文

1 有一个农夫，他的园子里有一棵苹果树。这棵苹果树不能结果，只能为麻雀和蝉提供一个可以栖息的地方，让他们坐在枝丫上叽叽喳喳。农夫很失望，决定把它砍掉。麻雀和蝉看到后，便请求他留下这棵树，“如果你砍掉这棵树，我们还得另外再找一个窝，而你也不会在干活时听到我们为你鼓劲的歌声了。”然而农夫没理睬他们，拿起斧头开始砍树，几斧下去之后，树上出

find, he threw down his axe, saying, "The old tree is worth keeping after all."

现一个洞并且发现了一个满是蜂蜜的蜂巢。他高兴地连忙抛下斧头说："这棵树还真是值得保留下来。"

provide [prəˈvaɪd] *v.* 提供
shelter [ˈʃeltə] *n.* 栖息地
sparrow [ˈspærəʊ] *n.* 麻雀
cicada [sɪˈkɑːdə] *n.* 蝉
chirp [tʃɜːp] *v.* （鸟）吱喳而鸣
refuse [rɪˈfjuːzd] *v.* 拒绝
delight [dɪˈlaɪt] *v.* 高兴
axe [æks] *n.* 斧

The Woman and the Farmer

女人和农夫

读一读，想一想

1. 农夫第一次哭泣是真心的吗？为什么？
2. 农夫第二次失声痛哭是为了什么？
3. 你觉得农夫是一个怎样的人？

精彩故事欣赏

1 A woman, who had lately lost her husband, used to go everyday to his grave and lament. A farmer, who ploughed not far from the spot, desired to marry her. So he left his plough, sat by her side and began to shed tears. She asked him why he swept, and he replied, " I have lost my wife, who was very dear to me ,and tears might divide my grief." "And I " said the woman "have lost my husband." And so for a while they mourned in silence .Then he said," Since you and I are in like case, shall we not do well to marry and live together? I shall take the place of your dead husband, and

译文

1 有一个女人刚刚失去了丈夫，她每天都要到丈夫的坟上痛哭。一个总是在不远处耕地的农夫想娶她为妻。于是，农夫放下自己的犁，来到她身边坐下，也痛哭了起来。女人问他为什么哭，农夫回答说："我的妻子死了，我非常爱她，也许眼泪能够减轻我的悲伤。"女人说："我丈夫也是刚刚去世。"两人就这样默然哀伤了一阵子。接着，农夫说：

you that of my dead wife." The woman agreed with him. Meanwhile, a thief had come and stolen the farmer's plough. On discovering the theft, he beat his breast and loudly bewailed. When the woman heard his cries, she came and said: "Why are you still sweeping?" To which he replied, "Yes, and I mean it this time."

"既然你我遭遇相同，我们为何不结为夫妻，在一起生活呢？我代替你死去的丈夫而你代替我死去的妻子。"女人同意了。这时候，有一个贼偷走了农夫的犁。看到自己的犁被偷了，农夫不禁捶胸顿足，大声痛哭。女人听见了他的哭声后走过来问道："你为什么还在哭呢？"农夫回答："是的，这一次是真心的。"

阅读无障碍

lately [ˈleɪtlɪ] *adv.* 不久前
grave [greɪv] *n.* 坟墓
lament [ləˈment] *v.* 哀悼
plough [plaʊ] *v.* 犁地
grief [gri:f] *n.* 忧伤
mourn [mɔ:n] *v.* 哀悼
meanwhile [ˈmi:nwaɪl] *adv.* 同时
bewail [bɪˈweɪl] *v.* 痛哭

The Boy and the Filberts

男孩和榛子

读一读，想一想

1. 男孩为什么哭？
2. 如果你是这个男孩，你会怎么做？

精彩故事欣赏

1 A boy put his hand into a jar of filberts, and grasped as many as he could possibly hold. But when he tried to pull out his hand, he was prevented from doing so by the neck of the jar. Unwilling to lose his nuts but unable to withdraw his hand, he burst into tears. A bystander said to him, "Be satisfied with half the quantity, and you'll be able to get your hand out without difficulty."

译文

1 一个小男孩把手伸进装满榛子的瓶子中，用尽全力去抓一大把。但当他想要缩回手时，却被瓶口挡住了。他既不想放弃手里的榛子，又不能拿出手来，于是大哭起来。一个旁观者对他说："还是知足些吧，若是拿一半，你的手就很容易出来了。"

阅读无障碍

jar [dʒɑː] *n.* 罐
hold [həʊld] *v.* 持有
unwilling [ʌnˈwɪlɪŋ] *adj.* 不情愿的
withdraw [wɪðˈdrɔː] *v.* 收回
bystander [ˈbaɪstændə] *n.* 旁观者
satisfied [ˈsætɪsfaɪd] *adj.* 感到满意的
quantity [ˈkwɒntɪtɪ] *n.* 数量
difficulty [ˈdɪfɪk(ə)ltɪ] *n.* 困难

The Man and the Lion

人和狮子

读一读，想一想

1. 狮子与人因为什么争论？
2. 人真的比狮子强大吗？为什么？

精彩故事欣赏

1 A man and a lion traveled together through the forest. They soon began to boast to each other. As they were disputing, they past a statue of some lions conquered by a man. The man pointed at it and said: "Look, how strong we are, and how we prevail over even the king of beasts." The lion replied: "This statue was made by one of you men. If we lions knew how to erect statues, you would see the man placed under the paw of the lion."

译 文

1 有一天，狮子与人一同穿越森林，不久他们就开始互相吹嘘。在争论不休之际，他们看见一块雕像，上面刻着一个人征服几只狮子的画面。那人指着雕像说："你看，我们是多么强大啊，连百兽之王都能战胜。"狮子回答道："如果我们狮子也知道怎样修建雕像，你便会看见人被压在狮子的爪下了。"

阅读无障碍

through [θruː] *prep.* 穿过
forest [ˈfɒrɪst] *n.* 森林
boast [bəʊst] *v.* 夸口
dispute [dɪˈspjuːt] *v.* 争论
conquer [ˈkɒŋkə] *v.* 战胜
point [pɒɪnt] *v.* 指向
prevail [prɪˈveɪl] *v.* 战胜，获胜
statue [ˈstætjuː] *n.* 雕像

The Traveller and His Dog

旅人和他的狗

读一读，想一想

1. 这个故事给我们什么启发？
2. 狗为什么打哈欠？

精彩故事欣赏

1 A traveller was about to start on a journey, and said to his dog, who was stretching himself by the door, "What are you yawning for? Hurry up and get ready, I mean you to go with me." But the dog merely wagged his tail and said quietly, "I'm ready, master. It's you I'm waiting for."

译文

1 一个旅人正准备出发，于是对着在门口伸懒腰的狗说："你还站在那里打什么呵欠呀？快点准备好，你要和我一起走！"但是狗摇着尾巴平静地说："我早就准备好了，一直在等你呢。"

阅读无障碍

start [stɑːt] *v.* 出发

journey [ˈdʒɜːnɪ] *n.* 旅行

stretch [stretʃ] *v.* 伸展

yawn [jɔːn] *v.* 打哈欠

hurry up 赶快

ready [ˈredɪ] *adj.* 准备好

merely [ˈmɪəlɪ] *adv.* 仅仅

wag [wæg] *v.* 摇摆

The Shipwrecked Man and the Sea 遇难者与海

读一读，想一想

1. 从这个故事你能体会到什么？
2. 旅人为什么责怪大海？
3. 你觉得大海应该被责怪吗？为什么？

1 A shipwrecked man cast up on the beach fell asleep after his struggle with the waves. When he woke up, he bitterly censured the sea for treachery in deceiving men with its smooth and smiling surface. Then, it turned in fury upon ships and sailors and sent them to destruction. The sea arose in the form of a woman, and replied, "Do not lay the blame on me, but on the winds. By nature I am as calm and safe as the land. But the winds fall upon me with their gusts and lash me into a fury, that is not natural to me."

1 一个遇上海难的人在风浪里经过一番挣扎，终于被冲上岸，在沙滩上睡着了。当他醒过来后，便愤然指责大海总以平静、温和的外表欺骗人们，然后却变得残暴，导致船只和船员的毁灭。这时，大海以女人的形象出现了，并且对他说："别责怪我，应该责怪风！我本身和大陆一样平静安全，但是只要狂风刮过，就会掀起惊涛骇浪，这并不是我的本性啊。"

fall asleep 入睡

struggle [ˈstrʌgl] *n.* 挣扎

bitterly [ˈbɪtəlɪ] *adv.* 苦涩地，悲痛地

censure [ˈsenʃə] *v.* 责难，责备

treachery [ˈtretʃ(ə)rɪ] *n.* 背叛；变节

deceiving [dɪˈsiviŋ] 欺骗；行骗（deceive 的 ing 形式）

destruction [dɪˈstrʌkʃ(ə)n] *n.* 破坏，毁灭

gust [gʌst] *n.* 一阵狂风

fury [ˈfjʊərɪ] *n.* 狂怒；暴怒

natural [ˈnætʃ(ə)r(ə)l] *adj.* 天生的

The Eagle and His Captor

鹰与捕鹰者

读一读，想一想

1. 鹰要把兔子送给谁？
2. 抓住鹰的人为什么要剪断他的翅膀？
3. 你同意狐狸的话吗？

精彩故事欣赏

1 A man once caught an eagle, he immediately clipped his wings and put him into his hen-house with the other fowls, at which treatment the eagle was very dejected and forlorn. Later the captor sold the eagle to a neighbor, who took him home and let his wings grow again. The eagle took flight, pounced upon a hare and brought it as an offering to his benefactor at once. A fox observed this and said to him, " Don't waste your gifts on him! Go and give them to the man who first caught you and make him your friend. And then

译　文

1 从前，有一个人捉住了一只鹰，他立即剪断了鹰的翅膀，把它放入鸡窝中与其他家禽一起饲养，鹰非常沮丧和绝望。没过多久，捕获老鹰的那个人将它卖给了一个邻居，邻居把鹰带回家后又帮它长出了新的翅膀。鹰飞出去抓住了一只兔子，立刻带回家给恩人。一只狐狸看到后，便对老鹰说：“不要把你的礼物浪费在他身

perhaps he won't catch you and clip your wings the second time."

上，把这份礼物送给以前捕获你的那个人，和他成为朋友。那么，或许他就不会再抓你并剪断你的翅膀了。"

阅读无障碍

clip [klɪp] *v.* 剪掉
fowl [faʊl] *n.* 家禽
dejected [dɪˈdʒektɪd] *adj.* 沮丧的
forlorn [fəˈlɔːn] *adj.* 绝望的
pounce [paʊns] *v.* 猛扑
benefactor [ˈbenɪfæktə] *n.* 恩人
observe [əbˈzɜːv] *v.* 观察
perhaps [pəˈhæps] *adv.* 或许

The Blacksmith and His Dog

铁匠与小狗

读一读，想一想

1. 铁匠为什么对小狗生气？
2. 你同意铁匠的话吗？

精彩故事欣赏

1 A blacksmith had a little dog, which used to sleep when his master was at work, but was very awake when it was time for meals. One day his master pretended to be disgusted at this, and then he had thrown him a bone, he said, "What on earth is the good of a lazy cur like you? When I am hammering away at my anvil, you just curl up and go to sleep, but as soon as I stop for a mouthful of food , you wag your tail to ask to be fed."

译　文

1 铁匠家有一条小狗，小狗经常在主人干活时睡觉，但是一到了吃饭时间，便非常清醒。有一天，铁匠假装对此很生气，扔给小狗一块骨头，说："地球上还有像你一样懒惰的杂狗吗？当我在铁砧上卖力工作时，你就知道蜷缩起来睡觉，可是，只要我一停下来吃点东西，你就摇着尾巴过来讨饭吃。"

阅读无障碍

master [ˈmɑːstə] *n.* 主人
awake [əˈweɪk] *adj.* 醒着的
pretend [prɪˈtend] *v.* 假装
disgusted [dɪsˈgʌstɪd] *adj.* 厌烦的
hammer [ˈhæmə] *v.* 锤击
anvil [ˈænvɪl] *n.* 铁砧
mouthful [ˈmaʊθfʊl] *n.* 一口之量
wag [wæg] *v.* 摇摆
tail [teɪl] *n.* 尾巴

The Ass and the Old Peasant 驴和老农夫

1. 老农民为什么要逃走？
2. 驴子想要跟着农民逃走吗？
3. 这个故事告诉了我们什么道理？

精彩故事欣赏

1 An old peasant was sitting in a meadow watching his ass, which was grazing. All of a sudden he saw a group of armed men stealthily approaching. He jumped up immediately, and begged the ass to run away with him as fast as possible. "Or else," said he, "we shall both be captured by them." But the ass just looked round lazily and said, "And if so, do you think they'll make me carry heavier loads than I have to now?" "No," said his master. "Oh well, then," said the ass, "I don't mind if they do get me, for I won't be any worse off."

译文

一位老农民坐在草地上看着他的驴吃草。突然他看到一群全副武装的人们正悄悄走近，便立刻跳了起来，恳求驴子跟他一起尽快逃走。“否则，”他说，“我们便会被他们逮住。”驴只是懒懒地看了看，说道：“如果这样的话，你认为他们会让我驮更重的东西吗？”“不，”主人说。“哦，这样的话，”驴子说，“我不介意他们把我抓走，因为我不会比现在的情况更糟糕。”

阅读无障碍

meadow [ˈmedəʊ] *n.* 草地

graze [greɪz] *v.* 吃草

armed [ɑːmd] *adj.* 武装的

stealthily [ˈstelθɪlɪ] *adv.* 暗地里

immediately [ɪˈmiːdiətli] *adv.* 立即

capture [ˈkɑːbən] *v.* 俘获

lazily [ˈleɪzɪlɪ] *adv.* 懒散地

load [ləʊd] *n.* 负载

The Impostor
说谎的人

1. 病人用什么供奉众神?
2. 众神是怎样惩罚这个人的?
3. 你觉得众神做得对吗?

精彩故事欣赏

1 A man fell ill and was in a very bad way, he made a vow that he would sacrifice a hundred oxen to the gods if they would allow him to be healthy again. Wishing to see if he would keep his vow, the gods made him recover in a short time. But in fact the man didn't even have one ox, so he made a hundred of little oxen made of tallow and offered them up on an altar, and said, "Ye gods, I call you to witness that I have kept my words." The gods determined to punish him, so they sent him a dream, in which he was told to go to the seashore and fetch a hundred of crowns. Hastening

译 文

1 有个人病的非常严重，他向众神发誓，如果能让他再次恢复健康，他一定会供奉一百头牛给众神。众神想要看看是否他能遵守诺言，便很快使他痊愈了。但事实上，这个人连一头牛都没有，于是，他就用牛油做成了一百头小牛，放到祭台上供奉给众神，说："神灵们，我请你们来见证，我已经遵守了我的诺言。"众神决定要惩罚他，便带他到一

in great excitement to the shore, he fell in with a band of robbers, who seized him and carried him off to sell as a slave. They sold him a hundred of crowns which was the sum he should fetch.

个梦境，在梦里，他被告知去海边可以得到100个银元。他怀着激动的心情急忙跑到海边可是却遇到一伙强盗，强盗抓住他并将他卖了去当奴隶，正好卖了他原本想得到的100银元。

阅读无障碍

vow [vaʊ] *n.* 发誓
sacrifice [ˈsækrɪfaɪs] *v.* 献祭
tallow [ˈtæləʊ] *n.* 牛脂
altar [ˈɔːltə] *n.* 祭坛
hasten [ˈheɪs(ə)n] *v.* 加速
excitement [ɪkˈsaɪtmənt] *n.* 兴奋
seize [siːz] *v.* 抓住
sum [sʌm] *n.* 金额

The Farmer and His Dogs
农场主和他的狗

读一读，想一想

1. 农夫为什么没有东西吃？
2. 农夫一共杀了多少种动物？
3. 这个故事给了我们什么启示？

精彩故事欣赏

1 A farmer was stuck in his farmstead by a severe storm, and was unable to go out and procure food for himself and his family. So he first killed his sheep to eat. As the storm still continued, he killed his goats. And last of all, as the weather showed no signs of subsiding, he was compelled to kill his oxen and eat them. When his dogs saw the animals being killed and eaten in turn, they said to one another, "We had better get out of this or we shall be the next to be killed!"

译 文

1 一个农夫被一场突如其来的暴风雪困在自己的农场里，无法外出为自己和家人获得食物。无奈之下，他先杀死了自己的绵羊来充饥。可是风暴依然持续不停，他又杀死了山羊。最后，因为风暴丝毫没有减弱的迹象，他又被迫杀死了自己的牛来吃。当他的狗看到动物们依次被吃掉后，便互相说："我们最好快点离开这里，不然就会成为下一个被杀的对象。"

阅读无障碍

stuck [stʌk] *adj.* 被困住的

farmstead [ˈfɑːmsted] *n.* 农庄

unable [ʌnˈeɪbəl] *adj.* 无能力的

procure [prəˈkjʊə] *v.* 获得

goat [gəʊt] *n.* 山羊

subsiding [səbˈsaɪd] *n.* 下沉

compel [kəmˈpel] *v.* 强迫

oxen [ˈɒksn] *n.* 公牛（ox 的复数）

The Butcher and His Customers 屠夫和他的顾客

读一读，想一想

1. 两个人怎样怎样偷屠夫的肉？
2. 屠夫是怎样知道他的肉被偷了？
3. 屠夫相信那两个小偷的话吗？

精彩故事欣赏

1 Two men were buying meat at a butcher's stall. When the butcher's back was turned for a moment, one of them snatched up a joint and thrust it under the other's cloak hurriedly, where it could not be seen. When the butcher turned round, he noticed the lost meat at once, and charged them with stealing it. But both of the two men said that they hadn't taken the meat, The butcher made sure they were deceiving him, but he only said, "You may cheat me with your lying, but you can't cheat the gods, and they won't let you off so lightly."

译 文

1 两个人正在屠户的摊位上买肉，当屠夫刚一转身背向他们的时候，其中一人便抓起一块猪肘，急忙放进另一个人的斗篷里，谁也看不到猎时我在斗篷里。当屠夫转过身来后，他立刻注意到少了一块肉，便指控他们偷了肉。但是这两个人都说没有拿。屠夫确信他们是在欺骗自己，但他只是说："你们可以用谎言来欺骗我，但却骗不了神，他们不会这么轻易放过你们的。"

阅读无障碍

stall [stɔːl] *n.* 货摊

snatch [snætʃ] *v.* 抢走

joint [dʒɔɪnt] *n.* 大块肉

cloak [kləʊk] *n.* 斗篷

hurriedly [ˈhʌrɪdlɪ] *adv.* 匆忙地

charge [tʃɑːdʒ] *v.* 控诉

steal [stiːl] *v.* 偷窃

deceive [dɪˈsiːv] *v.* 欺骗

cheat [tʃiːt] *v.* 欺骗

The Quack Doctor
江湖郎中

读一读，想一想

1. 病人的病很严重吗？
2. 死神为什么要起诉所有医生呢？
3. 病人最后一个咨询的医生是一位好医生吗？

精彩故事欣赏

1 A man fell ill and was completely bedridden. He consulted a number of doctors who all told him that his life was in no immediate danger, but his illness would probably last a grace time. Only the last one took a different view who advised him to prepare for the worst, " You have less than twenty-four hours to live," said he, "and I fear I can do nothing." As it turned out, he was totally wrong. After a few days, the sick man could quit his bed and took a walk outside. In the course of his walk, he met the doctor who had predicted his death. "Dear me" said the latter. "how do you

译　文

1 有一个人生病了，卧床不起。他咨询了很多医生，大多数医生都说这个病没有什么危险，但却需要持续一段时间才能好。只有最后一个医生给出了不同的观点，建议他做最坏的打算："你已经活不过明天了，"医生说，"恐怕我也帮不上什么忙。"然而事实证明这个医生完全错了。过了些日子，病人能够下床外出走动了。在路上，他又遇到了那

do ? You are fresh from the other world, no doubt. How are you departed friends getting on there?" "Very comfortable," replied the other, "for they have drunk the water of oblivion, and have forgotten all the troubles of life. By the way, just before I left, the authorities were making arrangements to prosecute all the doctors, because they won't let sick man die in the course of nature, but use their arts to keep them alive. But I persuaded them to let you off, for you were not a doctor, but a mere impostor."

个宣判他死期将至的医生。医生问他："哎呀，感觉如何？毫无疑问你从另一个世界回来了。那些死去的朋友怎么样？""非常舒服，"病人回答，"因为他们喝了忘情水，忘掉了生命中所有的烦恼，顺便一提，就在我离开前，死神正准备控告所有医生，因为他们没让病人自然死亡，而是利用他们的医术来挽救生命。原本你也在其中，但是我恳求他们放了你，因为你不是一个真正的医生，而仅仅是个江湖骗子而已。"

阅读无障碍

bedridden [ˈbedrɪd(ə)n] *adj.* 卧床不起的

consult [kənˈsʌlt] *v.* 咨询

advise [ədˈvaɪz] *v.* 建议

predict [prɪˈdɪkt] *v.* 预言

latter [ˈlætə] *adj.* 后面的

authority [ɔːˈθɒrɪtɪ] *n.* 当权者

arrangement [əˈreɪn(d)ʒm(ə)nt] *n.* 安排

prosecute [ˈprɒsɪkjuːt] *v.* 控告

persuade [pəˈsweɪd] *v.* 说服

The Miser
吝啬鬼

读一读，想一想

1. 吝啬鬼把金子藏在哪里？
2. 金子被谁偷走了？
3. 邻居给了吝啬鬼什么建议？

1 A miser sold all he had and bought a lump of gold, which he buried in a hole in the ground by the side of an old wall and went to look at it every day. One of his workmen observed his behavior and decided to watch his movements. He soon discovered the secret of the hidden treasure, so he excavated the hole and stole the gold. The miser found the hole empty and began to thump his chest and stamp his feet. A neighbor, seeing him overcome with grief and learning the cause, said, "Do not grieve so, but place a stone in the hole, and imagine that the gold is still lying there. It

1 一个吝啬鬼把自己所有的东西都卖掉了，换来一块金子。他把金子埋在一堵旧墙边上一个洞里，然后，每天都过去看一看那块金子。后来，吝啬鬼的一个工人发现了他的行为，于是留心观察，很快就发现了地下藏宝的秘密，所以他挖开了那个洞，把金子偷走了。吝啬鬼发现金子没了，伤心得捶胸顿足。一个邻居看到他伤心得快不行了，在了解了

will be the same to you. For when the gold was there, you had it not, as you did not make the slightest use of it."

事情的原由后对吝啬鬼说，"别那样伤心了，去找块石头放到那洞里面，把石头当成你的金子吧，那对你来说没什么区别。反正金子躺在那里，对你一点用都没有，跟石头一样。"

lump [lʌmp] *n.* 块
observe [əbˈzɜːv] *v.* 注意到
behavior [bɪˈheɪvjə] *n.* 行为
movement [ˈmuːvm(ə)nt] *n.* 活动
hidden [ˈhɪdn] *adj.* 隐藏的
excavate [ˈekskəveɪt] *v.* 挖掘
thump [θʌmp] *v.* 用拳头打
overcome [əʊvəˈkʌm] *v.* 克服
grief [griːf] *n.* 悲痛
slightest [ˈslaɪtɪst] *adj.* 极不重要的

The Man Who Lost His Spade 丢了铁锹的人

读一读，想一想

1. 这个人为什么要去寺庙？
2. 最后他找到偷铁锹的贼了吗？

1 A man was engaged in digging over his vineyard, and one day he missed his spade. Thinking it may have been stolen by one of his labourers, he questioned them closely, but they all denied. He was not convinced by their words ,and insisted that they should all go to the town and take oath in a temple that they were not guilty of the theft. Because he thought that the thief would not pass undetected by the shrewder gods. When they got inside the gate, the first thing they heard was the town crier proclaiming a reward for information about a thief who had stolen something from the temple. "Well," said the man to himself,

1 一个人在他葡萄园里翻土，有一天，他发现铁锹没了。他以为可能是被某个工人偷走了，就过去质问他们，但工人们都否认偷了铁锹。尽管工人们都否认了，可他依然不相信，坚持所有人都应该到城里的寺庙去发誓，证明自己没有犯盗窃罪。他以为小偷逃不过城里寺庙精明神灵的检测。但是他们走进大门听到的第一件事就是悬赏缉拿从寺庙偷东西的小偷。"好吧，"这个

" it strikes me I had better return home. If these town gods can't detect the thieves who stole from their own temples. It's scarcely likely they can tell me who stole my spade."

人自言自语地说，“这件事敲醒了我，我最好还是赶快回家吧。如果这些庙里的神都无法找到盗窃寺庙东西的贼，他们也不太可能告诉我是谁偷了我的铁锹。”

阅读无障碍

vineyard [ˈvɪnjɑːd] *n.* 葡萄园
labourer [ˈleɪb(ə)rə] *n.* 劳工
deny [dɪˈnaɪ] *v.* 否认
convince [kənˈvɪns] *v.* 相信
oath [əʊθ] *n.* 誓言
guilty [ˈgɪltɪ] *adj.* 有罪的
undetected [ʌndɪˈtektɪd] *adj.* 未被发现的
shrewd [ʃruːd] *adj.* 精明的
proclaim [prəˈkleɪm] *v.* 宣告
strike [straɪk] *v.* 打击
scarcely [ˈskɛrsli] *adv.* 几乎不，简直不

Grief and His Due
悲伤和他被指派的份额

读一读，想一想

1. 悲伤的份额是什么？
2. 这个故事告诉了我们什么道理？

1 When Jupiter was assigning the gods their privileges, it happened that grief was not present. But when all has received their share, he suddenly entered and asked for his due. Jupiter did not know what to do, for there was nothing left for him. However, at last he decided that he should belong to the tears. Thus it is the same with grief as it is with the other gods. The more devoutly men render to him his due, the more lavish is he of that which he has to bestow. It is not well, therefore, to mourn long for the departed. His sole pleasure is in such mourning.

1 朱庇特正在给神灵们分配特权，恰巧悲伤没有来。但是当所有的神灵都得到了他们的份额后，悲伤突然进来了，要求他应得的份额。朱庇特不知道怎么办，因为什么都没有留给他。然而，最后朱庇特决定，悲伤应该属于泪水。因此，悲伤与其他神灵一样，也得到了属于自己的份额。人们越虔诚的回报给悲伤，悲伤就会越发慷慨的赋予他们属于他的份额。所以，长久地为逝者悲伤并不好，悲伤的唯一乐趣就在这样的哀悼中。

阅读无障碍

assign [ə'saɪn] *v.* 分配
privilege ['prɪvɪlɪdʒ] *n.* 特权
present ['preznt] *adj.* 出席的
devoutly [di'vautli] *adv.* 虔诚地
lavish ['lævɪʃ] *adj.* 丰富的
bestow [bɪ'stəʊ] *v.* 授予
mourn [mɔːn] *v.* 哀痛
sole [səʊl] *adj.* 唯一的

The Two Soldiers and the Robber 两个士兵和强盗

读一读，想一想

1. 遇到抢劫时，两个士兵是怎么做的？
2. 那个先逃跑后又回来的士兵勇敢吗？
3. 这个故事说明了什么道理？

精彩故事欣赏

1 Two soldiers traveling together were set upon by a robber. The one fled away, the other stood his ground and defended himself with his stout right hand. The robber being slain, the timid companion ran up and drew his sword, and then, throwing back his traveling cloak said, "I'll at him, and I'll take care he shall learn whom he has attacked." On this, he who had fought with the robber made answer, "I only wish that you had helped me just now, even if it had been only with those words, for I should have been the more encouraged, believing them to be true;

译文

1 两个士兵一起赶路，途中遇上强盗打劫。其中一个马上逃躲到一边，另一个则坚守在原地用他强壮的右手勇敢地与强盗搏斗，很快就把强盗打得奄奄一息。这时，另外那个胆小的士兵跑过来，拔出剑，丢开外衣，大声喝道："我来对付他，我要让他知道，他抢劫的是什么人！"这时，那名勇敢的士兵说道："我希望你刚才能来帮助我，即使只是嘴上

but now put up your sword in its sheath and hold your equally useless tongue, till you can deceive others who do not know you. I, indeed, who have experienced with what speed you run away, know right well that no dependence can be placed on your valor."

说几句给我鼓鼓劲也好。我会更有勇气去战斗，因为我会相信你的话是真的。而现在，你还是将剑收回剑鞘，闭上嘴巴别光说没用的了。你只能欺骗那些不了解你的人，而我亲身经历了危险来临时你落荒而逃，非常清楚你的勇气是不可靠的。"

flee away 逃离
defend [dɪˈfend] *v.* 防御
stout [staʊt] *adj.* 强壮的
slay [sleɪ] *v.* 杀死
timid [ˈtɪmɪd] adj 胆小的
encourage [ɪnˈkʌrɪdʒ] *v.* 鼓舞
sheath [ʃiːθ] *n.* 鞘
deceive [dɪˈsiːv] *v.* 欺诈
dependence [dɪˈpendəns] *n.* 依赖
valor [ˈvælə] *n.* 勇猛

The Image-seller

卖神像的人

读一读，想一想

1. 这个人是怎样宣扬自己的神像的？
2. 神像真的能带给他好运吗？

精彩故事欣赏

1 A certain man made a wooden Image of Mercury, and exposed it for sale in the market. As no one offered to buy it, however, he would try to attract a purchaser by proclaiming the virtues of the Image. So he cried up and down the market, "A god for sale! A god for sale! One who'll bring you luck and keep you lucky!" Presently one of the bystanders stopped him and said, "If your god is all you make him out to be, how is it you don't keep him and make the most of him yourself?" "I'll tell you why," replied he, "he bring gain, it is true, but he takes his time about it; whereas I want money at once."

译 文

1 有个人刻了一尊墨丘利的木雕像，拿到市场上去卖。由于半天也没人来买，他觉得自己应该夸一夸这尊神像的价值，这样才能吸引购买者。于是，他四处走动着叫卖："卖神像了！卖神像了！一尊能带给你好运并保持好运的神像！"这时候，一个旁观者拦下他对他说道："如果你的神像真像你说的那样灵的话，你为什么不自己留着，充分利用他所能带给你的好处呢？""告诉你吧，”这个人回应道，“他肯定会给你带来好处，这千真万确，但这需要时间，而我需要得到现钱。”

阅读无障碍

expose [ɪkˈspəʊz] *v.* 使显露
purchaser [ˈpɜːtʃəsə(r)] *n.* 购买者
proclaim [prəˈkleɪm] *v.* 宣告
virtue [ˈvɜːtʃuː] *n.* 价值
up and down 到处
bystander [ˈbaɪstændə(r)] *n.* 旁观者
make the most of 充分利用
gain [ɡeɪn] *n.* 获益
whereas [ˌweərˈæz] *conj.* 然而

The Mother and the Wolf

母亲和狼

读一读，想一想

1. 狼为什么在林中小屋外等着?
2. 狼等到事物了吗?
3. 狼得到了什么样的教训?

精彩故事欣赏

1 A famished wolf was prowling about in the morning in search of food. As he passed the door of a cottage built in the forest, he heard a mother say to her child, "Be quiet, or I will throw you out of the window, and the wolf shall eat you." The wolf sat all day waiting at the door. In the evening he heard the same woman fondling her child and saying: "You are quiet now, and if the wolf should come, we will kill him." The wolf, hearing these words, went home, gasping with cold and hunger. When he reached his den, Mistress Wolf

译　文

1 一天早晨，一只饥饿的狼到处寻觅食物。当它经过一座林中小屋门前时，听到屋里一个母亲对小孩说："安静点，不准哭，不然我就把你扔到窗外去喂狼！狼信以为真，就坐在窗外等了整整一天。到了傍晚时分，它听到还是那个母亲，轻轻地爱抚着她的孩子："宝宝真乖！要是狼来了的话，我们就杀死它。"听到这些话，

inquired of him why he returned wearied and supperless, so contrary to his wont. He replied: “Why, forsooth because I gave credence to the words of a woman!”

狼倒抽了口气，恹恹地回家去了，又饿又冷。回到狼窝后，狼太太就问它怎么这副样子就回来了，看起来又累又饿的，和他平时不一样。它回答说：“哎，的确很糟糕！因为我轻易相信了那个女人的话！”

famished [ˈfæmɪʃt] *adj.* 非常饿的
prowl [praʊl] *v.* 徘徊
in search of 寻找
cottage [ˈkɒtɪdʒ] *n.* 村舍
fondle [ˈfɒndl] *v.* 爱抚
gasp [gɑːsp] *v.* 喘气
den [den] *n.* 兽穴
wearied [ˈwiərid] *adj.* 疲倦的
contrary [ˈkɒntrəri] *adv.* 相反地
wont [wəʊnt] *n.* 习惯
forsooth [fəˈsuːθ] *adv.* 确实
give credence to 相信

The Old Woman and the Wine-jar 老太婆和酒瓶

读一读，想一想

1. 老太婆为什么把酒闻了又闻？
2. 这个小故事给我们什么启示？

精彩故事欣赏

1 An old woman found an empty jar which had lately been full of prime old wine and which still retained the fragrant smell of its former contents. She greedily placed it several times to her nose, and drawing it backwards and forwards said, "O most delicious! How nice must the wine itself have been, when it leaves behind in the very vessel which contained it so sweet a perfume!"

译 文

1 一个老太婆捡到一个空酒瓶，不久前里面曾装过上好的陈酿，现在仍然还有浓浓的酒香飘出。她一次次把酒瓶放在鼻子下，来回晃动着，贪婪地嗅着酒香，并喃喃自语："真香啊！那酒真不知有多么香醇呢，连装过酒的空瓶子都留下这样浓郁甘美的香味。"

阅读无障碍

prime ['fæmɪʃt] *adj.* 最好的

retain [rɪ'teɪn] *v.* 保留

fragrant ['freɪgrənt] *adj.* 芳香的

greedily ['gri:dɪlɪ] *adv.* 贪婪地

vessel ['vesl] *n.* 容器

perfume ['pɜ:fju:m] *n.* 香味

The Soldier and His Horse

士兵和马

读一读，想一想

1. 战争期间士兵是怎样对待战马的？
2. 战争结束后士兵又是怎样对待战马的？
3. 士兵是个怎样的人？我们从中得到什么启示？

精彩故事欣赏

1 A soldier gave his horse a plentiful supply of oats in time of war, and tended him with the utmost care, for he wished him to be strong to endure the hardships of the field, and swift to bear his master, when need arose, out of the reach of danger. But when the war was over he employed him on all sorts of drudgery, bestowing but little attention upon him, and giving him, moreover, nothing but chaff to eat.

The time came when war broke out again, and the soldier saddled and bridled his horse, and, having put on his heavy coat of mail, mounted him to ride off and

译　文

1 战争期间，有个士兵每天都给自己的马喂充足的燕麦，精心地照料着他，希望他能身强体壮，在地形艰难的战场上驮着自己快速并持久地奔跑，从而使自己安全脱险。然而战争结束后，士兵却把马拉去做各种累活，一点也不再关照他，只给他喂谷糠。

后来战火重燃，士兵装上马鞍，套上笼头，穿上厚重的铠甲，跨上马背准备奔

take the field. But the poor half-starved beast sank down under his weight, and said to his rider, "You will have to go into battle on foot this time. Thanks to hard work and bad food, you have turned me from a horse into an ass, and you cannot in a moment turn me back again into a horse."

向战场。

但是马却毫无力气，根本承受不住，慢慢倒在地上，他对自己的主人说："这回，你得徒步去打仗了。你不断让我干苦役，却只给我谷糠吃，你已把我变成一头驴子，不能立刻把我变回马并当马骑了。"

阅读无障碍

plentiful [ˈplentɪfl] *adj.* 充裕的
oat [əʊt] *n.* 燕麦
tend [tend] *v.* 照料
utmost [ˈʌtməʊst] *adj.* 极度的
endure [ɪnˈdjʊə(r)] *v.* 忍耐
drudgery [ˈdrʌdʒəri] *n.* 苦工
bestow [bɪˈstəʊ] *v.* 给予
chaff [tʃɑːf] *n.* 谷糠
saddle [ˈsædl] *v.* 给（马）装鞍
bridle [ˈbraɪdl] *v.* 给……套笼头
mail [meɪl] *n.* 盔甲
mount [maʊnt] *v.* 骑上
half-starved [ˌhɑːfˈstɑːvd] *adj.* 半饿半饱的

The Oxen and the Butcher

公牛和屠夫

读一读，想一想

1. 公牛们为什么要杀死屠夫？
2. 老牛认为杀屠夫有用吗？
3. 这则寓言的启示是什么？

1 The oxen once upon a time sought to destroy the butchers, who practiced a trade destructive to their race. They assembled on a certain day to carry out their purpose, and sharpened their horns for the contest. But one of them who was exceedingly old (for many a field had he plowed) thus spoke: "These butchers, it is true, slaughter us, but they do so with skillful hands, and with no unnecessary pain. If we get rid of them, we shall fall into the hands of unskillful operators, and thus suffer a double death: for you may be assured, that though all the butchers should perish, yet will men never want beef."

1 一天，公牛想杀死屠夫，因为屠夫干的是屠杀他们的营生。他们聚在一起，商讨怎样执行计划才能达到目的。他们磨砺好自己的牛角，准备狠狠地对付屠夫。但是一头老牛（耕过许多田地）对大家说："那些屠夫确实宰杀我们，但他们在杀我们的时候用的是熟练的技巧，尽可能地使我们少受痛苦。如果我们除掉他们，我们就会落到那些没经验的

人手里，我们会死得更加痛苦。你们要知道，即使所有的屠夫都死了，人类也还是要吃牛肉的。”

seek [siːk] *v.* 谋求
destructive [dɪˈstrʌktɪv] *adj.* 毁灭性的
race [reɪs] *n.* 种族
assemble [əˈsembl] *v.* 集合
carry out 实施
purpose [ˈpɜːpəs] *n.* 目的
exceedingly [ɪkˈsiːdɪŋli] *adv.* 非常
slaughter [ˈslɔːtə(r)] *v.* 屠宰
skillful [ˈskɪlfʊl] *adj.* 熟练的
get rid of 除掉
perish [ˈperɪʃ] *v.* 死亡

The Prophet

算命人

读一读，想一想

1. 算命人为什么急忙往家赶？
2. 算命人真会算命吗？
3. 这个故事的寓意是什么？

精彩故事欣赏

1 A prophet sat in the market-place and told the fortunes of all who cared to engage his services. Suddenly there came running up one who told him that his house had been broken into by thieves, and that they had made off with everything they could lay hands on. He was up in a moment, and rushed off, tearing his hair and calling down curses on the miscreants. The bystanders were much amused, and one of them said, "Our friend professed to know what is going to happen to others, but it seems he's not clever enough to perceive what's in store for himself."

译 文

1 一个算命人在市场里摆摊，坐在那里专门给人算命。突然，有个人跑过来告诉他，他家进贼了，小偷带了所有能带走的，逃之夭夭了。一听到这个消息，算命人一下子跳起来，急忙往家赶，一边揪着头发一边咒骂小偷。旁观者都被逗笑了，其中一人说："我们的朋友声称自己能给别人预测未来，可是看上去他还不够聪明，对自己身上将要发生的事却预料不到！"

engage [ɪnˈgeɪdʒ] *v.* 吸引住

make off 逃走

rush off 仓促跑掉

curse [kɜːs] *n.* 咒骂

miscreant [ˈmɪskriənt] *n.* 歹徒

amused [əˈmjuːzd] *adj.* 被逗笑的

perceive [pəˈsiːv] *v.* 察觉

in store 将要发生

The Three Tradesmen

三个手艺人

读一读，想一想

1. 居民们聚在一起干什么？
2. 三个手艺人的提议有什么不同？为什么？

精彩故事欣赏

1 A great city was besieged, and its inhabitants were called together to consider the best means of protecting it from the enemy. A bricklayer earnestly recommended bricks as affording the best material for an effective resistance. A carpenter, with equal enthusiasm, proposed timber as a preferable method of defense. Upon which a currier stood up and said, "Sirs, I differ from you altogether: there is no material for resistance equal to a covering of hides; and nothing so good as leather."

译文

1 一座大城被敌人包围了，城中的居民们被召集在一起，商议最好的抗敌办法。一个砖瓦匠极力主张用砖块，认为砖块是最有效的抵御材料；一个木匠同样热情高涨，提议用木头来作为最合适的材料；紧接着，一个制革匠站起来说："先生们，我不同意你们的意见。依我看，作为防御的材料，没有任何东西比皮革更好了。"

besiege [bɪˈsiːdʒ] *v.* 包围

bricklayer [ˈbrɪkleɪə(r)] *n.* 砖匠

recommend [ˌrekəˈmend] *v.* 建议

material [məˈtɪəriəl] *n.* 材料

effective [ɪˈfektɪv] *adj.* 有效的

resistance [rɪˈzɪstəns] *n.* 抵抗

enthusiasm [ɪnˈθjuːziæzəm] *n.* 热情

timber [ˈtɪmbə(r)] *n.* 木材

currier [ˈkʌrɪə] *n.* 制革匠

leather [ˈleðə(r)] *n.* 皮革

The Trumpeter Taken Prisoner 被捕的号兵

读一读，想一想

1. 号兵觉得自己应该被宽恕的理由是什么？
2. 敌人为什么不宽恕号兵？
3. 这个故事告诉我们什么道理？

精彩故事欣赏

1 A trumpeter was captured by his enemy in a battle. When they were about to kill him, he begged them to have mercy on him. "I am not a warrior," said he. "I only blow the trumpet. It cannot harm you, then why should you kill me?" "You may not fight with a weapon," said the others, "but you encourage and guide your men to the fight."

译 文

1 有个号兵在一场战争中被敌人俘获了。在他们正要杀死他时，他求他们饶他一命。"我并不是个战士，"他大喊，"我只是个吹号的。它并不能伤人，你们为什么要杀死我呢？""你或许并没有用武器战斗，"敌人对他说道，"但是你却召集并鼓动其他士兵来攻打我们。"

阅读无障碍

captured [ˈkæptʃə(r)] *v.* 包围

have mercy on 开恩

warrior [ˈwɒriə(r)] *n.* 战士

weapon [ˈwepən] *n.* 武器

Venus and the Cat
维纳斯和猫

读一读，想一想

1. 猫为什么想变成人？
2. 维纳斯为什么把姑娘又变回了猫？
3. 这个小故事是否说明“江山易改，本性难移”？

精彩故事欣赏

1 A cat fell in love with a handsome young man, and entreated Venus to change her into the form of a woman. Venus consented to her request and transformed her into a beautiful damsel, so that the youth saw her and loved her, and took her home as his bride. While the two were reclining in their chamber, Venus wishing to discover if the cat in her change of shape had also altered her habits of life, let down a mouse in the middle of the room. The cat, quite forgetting her present condition, started up from the couch and pursued the mouse, wishing to eat it. Venus was much

译　文

1 一只猫爱上了一个英俊的青年，就去恳求维纳斯把她变成一个女子。维纳斯恩准了她的请求，把她变成了一个十分美丽的少女。青年对她一见钟情，便把她娶回了家。一天，维纳斯想去看看这只猫外形改变后生活习性是否也改变了，于是趁小两口倚坐在房间的时候，把一只老鼠放进了屋中。一见到老鼠，这位女子顿时忘了自己现在的身份，从沙发

disappointed and again caused her to return to her former shape.

上一跃而起，向老鼠扑了过去，要吃掉它。维纳斯对她非常失望，又把她变回了原来的样子。

阅读无障碍

entreat [ɪnˈtriːt] *v.* 恳求
form [fɔːm] *n.* 外形
consent [kənˈsent] *v.* 准许
transform [trænsˈfɔːm] *v.* 改变
damsel [ˈdæmzl] *n.* 少女
recline [rɪˈklaɪn] *v.* 倚靠
chamber [ˈtʃeɪmbə(r)] *n.* 房间
couch [kaʊtʃ] *n.* 沙发
pursue [pəˈsjuː] *v.* 追捕

The Archer and the Lion

射手和狮子

读一读，想一想

1. 神射手进山后，野兽们都是怎么做的？
2. 狮子为什么逃走？
3. 这个小故事给我们什么经验教训？

1 An archer went up into the hills to get some sport with his bow, and all the animals fled at the sight of him with the exception of the lion, who stayed behind and challenged him to fight. But he shot an arrow at the lion and hit him, and said, “There, you see what my messenger can do: just you wait a moment and I'll tackle you myself.” The lion, however, when he felt the sting of the arrow, ran away as fast as his legs could carry him. A fox, who had seen it all happen, said to the lion, “Come, don't be a coward. Why don't you stay and

1 一个神射手到山里去打猎，所有的野兽一见到他，马上四散逃窜，只有狮子待在原地向他发出挑战。神射手一箭射中了狮子，说道：“这只是给你提个醒，你等着，看我怎么收拾你！”狮子忍着伤口的疼痛，竭力逃走了。一只狐狸目睹了这一切，对狮子说：“加油，别做懦夫！为什么不留在原地，和他决战到底呢？”而

show fight?" But the lion replied, "You won't get me to stay, not you. Why? when he sends a messenger like that before him, he must himself be a terrible fellow to deal with."

狮子却回应道："说得倒轻巧，让我留下，你怎么不？这个人射的一支箭都已经这么厉害了，他本人肯定更是不好对付。"

bow [bow] *n.* 弓
flee [fliː] *v.* 逃走
exception [ɪk'sepʃn] *n.* 例外
challenge ['tʃæləndʒ] *v.* 向……挑战
shoot [ʃuːt] *v.* 射击
messenger ['mesɪndʒə(r)] *n.* 信使
tackle ['tækl] *v.* 对付

The Charger and the Miller

战马和磨坊主

读一读，想一想

1. 战马为什么感到悲哀？
2. 磨坊主是怎样开导战马的？
3. 我们从这个寓言中能学到什么？

1 A charger, feeling the infirmities of age, was sent to work in a mill instead of going out to battle. But when he was compelled to grind instead of serving in the wars, he bewailed his change of fortune and called to mind his former state, saying, "Ah! Miller, I had indeed to go campaigning before, but I was barbed from counter to tail, and a man went along to groom me, and now I cannot understand what ailed me to prefer the mill before the battle." "Forbear," said the Miller to him, "harping on what was of yore, for it is the common lot of mortals to sustain the ups and downs of fortune."

1 有匹战马感到年老体衰，便选择离开战场，到一个磨坊工作。但是每当他不得不拉磨而不是像往日一样在战场上冲锋陷阵时，它就悲叹自己的不幸。他对磨坊主说："哎！过去我征战沙场，从头到脚锋芒毕露，还有专人照料我，而如今确是这个样子，我真不明白自己怎么就选择离开战场到磨坊来了呢。"磨场主对他说："别总是不停地唠叨过去，命运总是跌宕起伏的，你还是接受现实吧。"

阅读无障碍

infirmity [ɪn'fɜːməti] *n.* 衰弱
mill [mɪl] *n.* 磨坊
compel [kəm'pel] *v.* 强迫
grind [graɪnd] *v.* 磨碎
bewail [bɪ'weɪl] *v.* 悲哀
campaign [kæm'peɪn] *v.* 参战
groom [gruːm] *v.* 清洁
ail [eɪl] *v.* 折磨
forbear [fɔː'beə(r)] *v.* 忍耐
harp [hɑːp] *v.* 不停地说
sustain [sə'steɪn] *v.* 经受

The Father and His Two Daughters 父亲与女儿

读一读，想一想

1. 父亲的两个女儿为什么愿望不同？
2. 这个故事说明了什么？

精彩故事欣赏

1 A man had two daughters, the one married to a gardener, and the other to a tile-maker. After a time he went to the daughter who had married the gardener, and inquired how she was and how all things went with her. She said, “All things are prospering with me, and I have only one wish, that there may be a heavy fall of rain, in order that the plants may be well watered.” Not long after, he went to the daughter who had married the tile-maker, and likewise inquired of her how she fared. She replied, “I want for nothing, and have only one wish, that the dry weather may

译 文

1 一个人有两个女儿，一个嫁给了菜农，另一个嫁给了制瓦匠。过了些日子，他到嫁给菜农的女儿家里，询问女儿的情况，生活过得怎样。她说：“一切顺利，只希望能下一场大雨，好好地浇灌一下地里的蔬菜。”不久之后，他又到嫁给制瓦匠的女儿家里去，问了同样的问题。她回答说：“我不奢望什么，只求这干燥的天气能一直持续下去，炙热的阳光

continue, and the sun shine hot and bright, so that the bricks might be dried." He said to her, "If your sister wishes for rain, and you for dry weather, with which of the two am I to join my wishes?"

能尽快把砖头都晒干。"听了女儿的话，父亲对她说："你姐姐盼着下雨，而你却希望晴天，在你们两人的愿望中，我到底该希望你们哪个好呢？"

tile-maker [taɪl ˈmeɪkə(r)] *n.* 制瓦匠
prosper [ˈprɒspə(r)] *v.* 兴旺
likewise [ˈlaɪkwaɪz] *adv.* 同样地
fare [feə(r)] *v.* 进展

The Bee-keeper

养蜂人

读一读，想一想

1. 蜜蜂为什么刺养蜂人？
2. 生活中有像蜜蜂这样的人吗？他们应该怎么做？

精彩故事欣赏

1 A thief found his way into an apiary when the bee-keeper was away, and stole all the honey. When the keeper returned and found the hives empty, he was very much upset and stood staring at them for some time. Before long the bees came back from gathering honey, and, finding their hives overturned and the keeper standing, they made for him with their stings. At this he fell into a passion and cried, "You ungrateful scoundrels, you let the thief who stole my honey get off scot-free, and then you go and sting me who have always taken such care of you!"

译文

1 一个小偷趁养蜂人不在家，偷偷溜进养蜂场，偷走了所有的蜂蜜。当养蜂人回来后，他发现所有的蜂箱都空了。养蜂人极度伤心，站在那里盯着蜂箱一动不动。不久，蜜蜂采蜜回来，发现自己的蜂巢都被翻倒了，而养蜂人站在旁边，他们一窝蜂地涌向养蜂人，狠狠地刺他。养蜂人浑身难受地大喊道：“你们这群不知好歹的坏蛋！你们不去惩罚那些偷蜂蜜的贼，却刺伤我这个一直精心照顾你们的人！”

apiary [ˈeɪpiəri] *n.* 养蜂场

stare [steə(r)] *v.* 盯着看

before long 不久之后

overturn [ˌəuvəˈtɜːn] *v.* 翻倒

passion [ˈpæʃn] *n.* 受难

scoundrel [ˈskaʊndrəl]] *n.* 坏蛋

scot-free [ˈskɔtfriː] *adj.* 不受处罚的

The Weasel and the Man

黄鼠狼和人

读一读，想一想

1. 黄鼠狼为什么觉得自己应该被饶恕？
2. 我们应如何对待像黄鼠狼一样的人呢？

精彩故事欣赏

1 A man once caught a weasel, which was always sneaking about the house, and was just going to drown it in a tub of water, when it begged hard for its life, and said to him, "Surely you haven't the heart to put me to death? Think how useful I have been in clearing your house of the mice and lizards which used to infest it, and show your gratitude by sparing my life." "You have not been altogether useless, I grant you," said the man, "but who killed the fowls? Who stole the meat? No no! You do much more harm than good, and die you shall."

译 文

1 从前，有个人抓住了一只黄鼠狼，这只黄鼠狼总是在房子周围鬼鬼祟祟。这个人正要把黄鼠狼扔到水桶里淹死时，黄鼠狼苦苦哀求他饶自己一命，并且对他说："你肯定不忍心杀了我！想一想我是多有用吧，我帮你清理家里的老鼠和蜥蜴，为了表示你对我的感激，就饶了我吧。""我承认，你并非一无是处，"男人说，"但是，是谁杀了家禽？又是谁偷走了肉？不，我绝不会放过你！你做的坏事远远超过好事，你死有应得。"

weasel [ˈwiːzl] *n.* 黄鼠狼

sneaking [ˈsniːkɪŋ] *adj.* 偷偷摸摸的

tub [tʌb] *n.* 桶

have the heart to 忍心做

lizard [ˈlɪzəd] *n.* 蜥蜴

infest [ɪnˈfest] *v.* 寄生于

gratitude [ˈgrætɪtjuːd] *n.* 感激

fowl [faʊl] *n.* 家禽

The Farmer and the Fox

农夫和狐狸

读一读，想一想

1. 农夫为什么要报复狐狸？
2. 最终的结果是什么？
3. 这个寓言有什么启示？

精彩故事欣赏

1 A farmer, who bore a grudge against a fox for robbing his poultry yard, caught him at last, and being determined to take an ample revenge, tied some rope well soaked in oil to his tail, and set it on fire. The fox by a strange fatality rushed to the fields of the farmer who had captured him. It was the time of the wheat harvest, but the farmer reaped nothing that year and returned home grieving sorely.

译　文

1 农夫受够了狐狸总是来院子里偷他的家禽，最终想办法捉住了他。他决定狠狠地教训一下狐狸，就在狐狸尾巴上绑上一根泡过油的绳子，然后点上了火。天降横祸，狐狸难受地上蹿下跳，结果冲进了农夫的田地里。刚好麦收在即，结果却成了一片火海。最终农夫颗粒无收，后悔莫及。

阅读无障碍

grudge [grʌdʒ] *v.* 不满

poultry [ˈpəʊltri] *n.* 家禽

ample [ˈæmpl] *adj.* 足够的

revenge [rɪˈvendʒ] *n.* 报复

tie [taɪ] *v.* 系

soaked [səʊkt] *adj.* 浸泡的

fatality [fəˈtæləti] *n.* 灾祸

capture [ˈkæptʃə(r)] *v.* 俘获

reap [riːp] *v.* 收获

grieve [griːv] *v.* 伤心

sorely [ˈsɔːli] *adv.* 非常

The Lion in a Farmyard
农场里的狮子

读一读，想一想

1. 狮子闯进农场后，农夫是怎么做的？
2. 农夫付出的代价是什么？
3. 农夫是一个怎样的人？

精彩故事欣赏

1 A lion entered a farmyard. The farmer, wishing to catch him, shut the gate. When the lion found that he could not escape, he flew upon the sheep and killed them, and then attacked the oxen. The farmer, beginning to be alarmed for his own safety, opened the gate and released the lion. On his departure the farmer grievously lamented the destruction of his sheep and oxen, but his wife, who had been a spectator to all that took place, said, "On my word, you are rightly served, for how could you for a moment think of shutting up a lion along with you in your

译　文

1 一头狮子闯进了农场。农夫想抓住他，就关上了大门。狮子发现自己逃不掉了，就扑向了羊群，把羊都咬死后又朝公牛扑去。农夫这才担心起自己的生命安全来，赶紧打开大门，放走了狮子。狮子离开后，农夫看到毁了的羊群和牛，悲痛欲绝。但农夫的妻子，作为旁观者目睹了所发生的一切，对他说道："依我看，你这是活该！你怎么也不动动

farmyard when you know that you shake in your shoes if you only hear his roar at a distance?"

脑子，竟敢把狮子和自己关在农场里，平时你老远听到它的咆哮声，都会吓得双脚发软啊！"

be alarmed for 对……放心不下
release [rɪˈliːs] v. 释放
departure [dɪˈpɑːtʃə(r)] n. 离开
grievously [ˈgriːvəslɪ] adv. 悲伤地
lament [ləˈment] v. 痛惜
destruction [dɪˈstrʌkʃn] n. 破坏
spectator [spekˈteɪtə(r)] n. 旁观者
take place 发生
be rightly served 活该
at a distance 在远处

The Eagle and the Arrow

鹰和箭

读一读，想一想

1. 鹰发出什么感慨？

2. 鹰的悲惨遭遇给我们什么启示？

精彩故事欣赏

1 An eagle was flying in the sky. As soon as it saw a rabbit, it swooped down on its prey. Suddenly it was hit by an arrow. It fluttered slowly down to the earth, and blood was pouring from the wound. When the eagle looked down, he found that the shaft of the arrow was feathered with one of its own plumes. "Alas!" it cried. "We often give our enemies the means for our own destruction."

译 文

1 一只鹰在天空飞翔，突然看见一只野兔，就俯冲下来捕捉猎物。突然，它被一支箭射中。它慢慢扇动翅膀落到地上。鲜血从伤口喷涌而出。它低头发现这支箭的箭羽竟是它自己的羽毛，"哎，"鹰发出悲鸣："我们经常会给敌人提供毁灭我们自己的工具！"

阅读无障碍

swoop [swu:p] *v.* 俯冲

prey [preɪ] *n.* 猎物

flutter [ˈflʌtə(r)] *v.* 振翼

shaft [ʃɑ:ft] *n.* 柄

plume [plu:m] *n.* 羽毛

means [mi:nz] *n.* 工具

destruction [dɪˈstrʌkʃn] *n.* 毁灭

The Lioness and the Vixen

母狮与雌狐

读一读，想一想

1. 雌狐以什么为傲？
2. 母狮是怎样回应雌狐的？
3. 这个故事的寓意是什么？

精彩故事欣赏

1 One morning when a vixen was taking her babies out of the lair, she saw a lioness and her cub. "Why do you have only one child, dear dame?" asked the vixen. "Look at my healthy and numerous children here, and imagine, if you are able, how a proud mother should feel." The lioness said calmly, "Yes, just look at that beautiful collection. What are they? Foxes! I've only one, but remember, that one is a lion."

译 文

1 一天早晨，一只雌狐带着她的孩子们走出巢穴，看见一只母狮和她的孩子。"为什么你只有一个孩子呢，夫人？"雌狐问道，"看看我这一群孩子，个个健康强壮的，如果能养出这样一大群孩子的话，一个母亲会感到多么骄傲啊！"然而母狮却平静地说："是呀，看看这么漂亮的一大群，可他们都是什么呀？他们都是狐狸！我虽然只有一个，但请记住，他可是一头狮子！"

vixen [ˈvɪksn] *n.* 雌狐

lair [leə(r)] *n.*（野兽的）巢穴

cub [kʌb] *v.* 幼兽

dame [deɪm] *n.* 夫人

numerous [ˈnjuːmərəs] *adj.* 很多的

imagine [ɪˈmædʒɪn] *v.* 想象

collection [kəˈlekʃn] *n.* 一群

The River and the Sea

河流与大海

读一读，想一想

1. 河流为什么联合抵抗大海？
2. 大海怎样应对的？
3. 这个故事有什么启示？

精彩故事欣赏

1 Once upon a time all the Rivers combined to protest against the action of the Sea in making their waters salt.

2 "When we come to you," said they to the Sea, "we are sweet and drinkable, but when once we have mingled with you, our waters become as briny and unpalatable as your own." The Sea replied shortly, "Keep away from me and you'll remain sweet."

译　文

1 很久以前，所有的河流为了保护自己不变咸，就联合起来共同抵抗大海。

2 "原本我们流向你的时候是甘甜可口的，"河流一起责骂大海，"可一旦和你融合起来，就变得和你一样咸，根本没法再喝了。"大海听了后，只是淡淡地说："离我远点，别流到我这儿，那么你们依然还会清甜甘洌。"

阅读无障碍

drinkable [ˈdrɪŋkəbl] *adj.* 可饮用的

mingle [ˈmɪŋgl] *v.* 混合

briny [ˈbraɪni] *adj.* 咸的

unpalatable [ʌnˈpælətəbl] *adj.* 味道差的

The Wolf and the Lion

狼与狮子

读一读，想一想

1. 狼为什么抱怨？
2. 羊是狼合法得到的吗？
3. 从这个小故事中，我们可以学到什么？

精彩故事欣赏

1 A wolf, having stolen a lamb from a fold, was carrying him off to his lair. A lion met him in the path, and seizing the lamb, took it from him. Standing at a safe distance, the wolf exclaimed, "You have unrighteously taken that which was mine from me!" To which the lion jeeringly replied, "It was righteously yours, eh? The gift of a friend?"

译 文

1 一只狼从羊群中偷走一只羊，急忙叼着羊往回走。路上遇到了一头狮子。狮子立刻抓着小羊，把它从狼口里抢走了。狼只能干瞪眼，慢慢退到安全的距离，朝狮子抱怨道说："你这行为太不正当了，抢走属于我的东西。"那狮子嘲弄地说道："这么说，这只羊是你正当获得了？是朋友送你的？"

阅读无障碍

unrighteously [ʌnˈraɪtʃəslɪ] *adv.* 不正当地

jeeringly [dˈʒɪərɪŋlɪ] *adv.* 嘲弄地

righteously [ˈraɪtʃəslɪ] *adv.* 正当地

The Wasp and the Snake

黄蜂和蛇

读一读，想一想

1. 蛇为什么要把头伸到车轮下？
2. 这个故事有什么寓意？

精彩故事欣赏

1 A wasp seated himself upon the head of a snake, striking him unceasingly with his stings, wounded him to death. The snake, being in great torment and not knowing how to rid himself of his enemy, saw a wagon heavily laden with wood, and went and purposely placed his head under the wheels, saying, "At least my enemy and I shall perish together."

译　文

1 一只黄蜂坐在一条蛇的头上，不断地用刺去扎他，蛇都快被蜇死了。蛇疼痛难忍却怎么也赶不走他的仇敌。就在蛇绝望之际，他看见远处驶来一辆满载木材的马车，蛇于是故意将头伸到车轮下，对黄蜂说："就让我和仇敌同归于尽吧！"

阅读无障碍

unceasingly [ʌnˈsiːsɪŋlɪ] *adv.* 不断地

torment [ˈtɔːment] *n.* 痛苦

lade [leɪd] *v.* 装载

purposely [ˈpɜːpəsli] *adv.* 故意地

The Fox and the Grapes

狐狸和葡萄

读一读，想一想

1. 狐狸为什么要吃葡萄？
2. 最后他吃到葡萄了吗？
3. 你觉得狐狸是抱着怎样的心情说葡萄酸的呢？

精彩故事欣赏

1 One hot summer day a fox was walking through an orchard. He stopped before a bunch of grapes. They were ripe and juicy. "I'm just feeling thirsty." he thought. So he backed up a few paces, got a running start, jumped up, but could not reach the grapes. He walked back and jumped up again, but still, he missed the grapes. The fox tried over and over again but never succeeded. At last he decided to give up. He walked away with his nose in the air, and said, "I am sure they are sour."

译 文

1 一个炎热的夏日，一只狐狸走过一个果园。他在一大串熟透而多汁的葡萄前停下了。狐狸想："我正感觉口渴。"所以他后退了几步，向前一跑，跳起来，却无法够到葡萄。狐狸后退又跳了一次。但是仍然没有得到葡萄。狐狸试了一次又一次，都没有成功。最后，他决定放弃了，他昂着头离开，说道："我敢肯定这些葡萄是酸的。"

阅读无障碍

orchard [ˈɔːtʃəd] *n.* 果园

bunch [bʌntʃ] *n.* 串

ripe [raɪp] *adj.* 成熟的

juicy [ˈdʒuːsi] *adj.* 多汁的

pace [peɪs] *n.* 一步

succeed [səkˈsiːd] *v.* 成功

give up 放弃

sour [ˈsaʊə(r)] *adj.* 有酸味的

The Goose That Laid the Golden Eggs 下金蛋的鹅

读一读，想一想

1. 鹅每天下几个金蛋？
2. 这对夫妇为什么要杀掉鹅？
3. 是什么导致了夫妇最后的下场？

精彩故事欣赏

1 In a midnight, a goose raised by an old couple kept gabbling. The old couple got up to check and found their goose laid a golden egg. "It's great. Let's sell out the golden egg tomorrow and then we will have money." The old lady happily said. The next day, the old man sold out the egg and used the money to buy more food. Besides, he also bought better feed for the goose and hoped it could lay more golden eggs. However, the goose still laid one egg every day. The old couple couldn't wait. Thus, the old lady said, "Since she lays a

译 文

1 一天半夜，一对老夫妇养的鹅不停地叫。这对夫妇起床检查后发现他们的鹅下了一只金蛋。"太好了，让我们明天把金蛋卖了，这样我们就有钱了。"老太太开心地说。第二天，老头子把蛋卖了，买了更多食物，而且他还给鹅买了更好的饲料，希望她能下更多的金蛋。然而，这只鹅仍然每天只下一个金蛋。这对老夫妇

golden egg every day, there must be many golden eggs inside her. If we kill her and take out all the golden eggs, we could buy a big house and live a better life." The old man agreed with his wife, so they killed the goose. But there was no golden egg inside the goose. And because of their greed, the couple wouldn't have golden eggs to sell any more.

等不及了。因此老妇人说："既然她每天都下一只金蛋，她的肚子里肯定有更多。如果我们把鹅杀了，把她肚子里的金蛋都取出来，那我们就能买一栋大房子，过上更好的生活了。"老头子很赞同，所以他们把鹅杀了。但是鹅的肚子里一个金蛋都没有。而且，因为他们的贪婪，这对夫妇再也没有金蛋可以卖了。

阅读无障碍

raise [reɪz] *v.* 养育
gabble [ˈgæbl] *v.* 急促地叫
couple [ˈkʌpl] *n.* 夫妻
besides [bɪˈsaɪdz] *adv.* 此外
lay [leɪ] *v.* 下蛋
since [sɪns] *conj.* 既然
inside [ɪnˈsaɪd] *prep.* 在……之内
greed [griːd] *n.* 贪婪

The Cat and the Mice

猫和老鼠

读一读，想一想

1. 猫听到了什么消息？
2. 猫想出什么办法来骗老鼠？
3. 老鼠们最后上当了吗？

精彩故事欣赏

1 There was once a house that was overrun with mice. A cat heard of this, and said to herself, "That's the place for me." Then she went and stayed in the house, and caught the mice one by one and ate them. At last the mice could not stand it any more, and they determined to hide in their holes and stayed here. "That's awkward," said the cat, "the only thing to do is to coax them out by a trick." So she climbed up the wall and let herself hang down by her hind legs from a peg, and pretended to be dead. After a while a mouse peeped

译 文

1 从前有一座房子，里面的老鼠泛滥成灾。一只猫听到这个消息，便自言自语说："那正是适合我的地方。"于是她在那个房子住下了，然后一只接一只地抓老鼠，吃掉他们。最后，老鼠们再也受不了了，决定躲到洞里再也不出来了。"这下麻烦了，"猫说，"只能想个窍门把他们骗出来了。"她爬上墙，用后腿钩住木桩倒挂下

out and saw the cat hanging there. "Aha!" it cried, "You're very clever, madam, but even if you turn yourself into a bag of meal hanging there, you won't catch us coming anywhere near you."

来，假装已经死了。过了一会儿，一只老鼠向外偷看，看到正挂在那里的猫。"啊哈！"他大叫，"夫人，你还真聪明，不过，就算你假装成一袋食粮挂在那里，我们也不会去接近你让你抓住的。"

阅读无障碍

overrun [əʊvəˈrʌn] *n.* 泛滥成灾
stand [stænd] *v.* 忍受
coax [kəʊks] *v.* 哄骗
trick [trɪk] *n.* 诡计
hind [haɪnd] *adj.* 后部的
peg [peg] *n.* 桩
peep [piːp] *v.* 窥视
hang [hæŋ] *v.* 悬挂

The Mischievous Dog

恶狗

读一读，想一想

1. 客人们为什么讨厌狗？
2. 狗喜欢这个铃铛吗？
3. 主人为什么给狗戴上铃铛？

精彩故事欣赏

1 There was once a dog who often snapped at people and bit them without any reasons. Every one who came to his master's house was very sick of him . So his master fastened a bell round his neck to warn people. The dog was very proud of the bell, and strutted about tinkling it with satisfaction. But an old dog came up to him and said, "The lower profile you keep, the better for yourself. You think that your bell was a reward of merit? On the contrary, it is a badge of disgrace."

译　文

1 从前，有一条狗经常无故咬人，每个去他主人家做客的人都很讨厌他。所以主人在他的脖子上系上了一个铃铛来提醒人们。狗很骄傲有这个铃铛，于是带着它大摇大摆的走来走去，对铃铛声十分满意。但是，一条老狗走过来对他说："姿态越低，对你越有利。你以为这个铃铛是对你的奖赏吗？事实恰恰相反，它是耻辱的标志。"

阅读无障碍

snap [snæp] *v.* 猛咬

bite [baɪt] *v.* 咬

fasten [ˈfɑːs(ə)n] *v.* 系牢

strut [strʌt] *v.* 趾高气扬地走

tinkle [ˈtɪŋk(ə)l] *v.* 使发清脆的声响

profile [ˈprəʊfaɪl] *n.* 姿态

reward [rɪˈwɔːd] *n.* 奖励

merit [ˈmerɪt] *n.* 功绩

on the contrary 正相反

badge [bædʒ] *n.* 标记

disgrace [dɪsˈgreɪs] *n.* 耻辱

The Mice in Council

老鼠开会

读一读，想一想

1. 老鼠们想到了什么办法？
2. 这个办法可以实行吗？
3. 这个故事告诉了我们什么道理？

精彩故事欣赏

1 Once upon a time all the mice met together in council, and discussed the best means of securing themselves against the attacks of the cat. An experienced mouse got up and said, "I think I have hit upon a plan which will ensure our safety in the future. It is that we should fasten a bell round the neck of the cat, which will warn us of her approach by its tinkling." This proposal was warmly applauded, and it had been already decided to adopt it. When an old mouse got upon his feet and said, "I agree with you all that the plan before us is an admirable one, but may I ask who is

译　文

1 从前，所有的老鼠聚集在一起，开会讨论抵抗猫的攻击的最好方法。一只经验丰富的老鼠站起来，说："我忽然想到一个办法，可以确保大家将来的安全。我们应该在猫的脖子上系上一个铃铛，这样当他走近时，铃铛声会警告我们。"他的提议受到大家的热烈称赞，最后也决定采用这个办法。就在这时，一只年长的老鼠伸出他的爪子，说："我十分

going to bell the cat?"

赞同摆在我们面前这个绝妙的办法，但是，我能问一下谁去给猫系铃铛吗？"

阅读无障碍

council [ˈkaʊns(ə)l;] *n.* 会议

secure [sɪˈkjʊə] *v.* 保护

experienced [ɪkˈspɪərɪənst] *adj.*；富有经验的

safety [ˈseɪftɪ] *n.* 安全

fasten [ˈfɑːs(ə)n] *v.* 使固定

approach [əˈprəʊtʃ] *n.* 接近

tinkling [ˈtɪŋklɪŋ] *n.* 叮叮声

proposal [prəˈpəʊz(ə)l] *n.* 提议

applaud [əˈplɔːd] *v.* 赞同

admirable [ˈædm(ə)rəb(ə)l] *adj.* 值得赞扬的

The Bat and the Weasels

蝙蝠和黄鼠狼

读一读，想一想

1. 蝙蝠第一次被谁抓住了？
2. 蝙蝠第二次被谁抓住了？
3. 蝙蝠到底是老鼠还是鸟呢？

精彩故事欣赏

1 A bat which fell on the ground was caught by a weasel, and was going to be eaten. It begged the weasels to spare its life. The weasel said he couldn't do that because he was an enemy of all birds on principle. "Oh, but," said the bat, "I'm not a bird at all. I'm a mouse." "So you are," said the weasel, "now I come to look at you carefully." and he let it go. After a few days, the bat was caught by another weasel in the same way, and, as before, begged for its life. "No," said the weasel, "I never let a mouse go by any chance." "But I'm not a mouse," said the bat, "I'm a bird." "Oh, so

译　文

1 一只落在地上的蝙蝠被一只黄鼠狼捉住了，在快要被吃掉时，他请求黄鼠狼饶他一命。黄鼠狼说不能放了他，因为他本来就是所有鸟类的敌人。蝙蝠说："哦，但我根本不是鸟，"蝙蝠说，"我是只老鼠。"黄鼠狼说："原来你是老鼠呀，现在我才看清楚你。"于是，黄鼠狼放走了他。不久，蝙蝠又以同样的方式被另一只黄鼠狼捉住了，并且像从前

you are," said the weasel, and he let the bat go too.

一样，他乞求黄鼠狼放了自己。“不行，”黄鼠狼说，“我绝不可能放过任何一只老鼠。”“可是我不是老鼠呀，”蝙蝠说，“我是一只鸟儿。”“哦，原来你是一只鸟儿呀！”黄鼠狼说着，也把他放走了。

阅读无障碍

ground [graʊnd] *n.* 地面
beg [beg] *v.* 恳求
spare [speə] *v.* 饶恕
enemy [ˈenimi] *n.* 仇敌
principle [ˈprɪnsɪp(ə)l] *n.* 原则
mouse [maʊs] *n.* 老鼠
carefully [ˈkeəfəlɪ] *adv.* 小心谨慎地
chance [tʃɑːns] *n.* 机会

The Dog and the Sow

狗和母猪

读一读，想一想

1. 母猪为什么觉得自己的孩子更好?
2. 你觉得母猪的话对吗？为什么？

精彩故事欣赏

1 A dog and a sow were arguing and each claimed that its own young ones were finer than those of any other animal. "Well," said the sow at last, "mine can see, at any rate, when they come into the world, but yours are born blind."

译 文

1 一只狗和一只母猪正在互相争辩，它们都认为自己的孩子比任何其他的动物的孩子更加出色。“嗯，”最后母猪说，“至少我的孩子一生下来就能看见东西，而你的孩子生下来就是瞎的！”

阅读无障碍

argue [ˈɑːgjuː] *v.* 争论
claim [kleɪm] *v.* 声称
own [əʊn] *adj.* 自己的
at last 最后
at any rate 至少
born [bɔːn] *adj.* 天生的
blind [blaɪnd] *adj.* 瞎的

The Fox and the Crow

狐狸和乌鸦

读一读，想一想

1. 狐狸为什么赞美乌鸦？
2. 乌鸦上当了吗？
3. 这个故事告诉了我们什么道理？

精彩故事欣赏

1 A crow stood in a tree. She had a big piece of cheese in her beak. A fox came and saw the crow and her cheese. He said, "What a beautiful bird! What beautiful eyes! What beautiful feathers! I wonder if she has got a beautiful voice! "The crow opened her mouth and sang, "Caw, caw!" At the same time, the big piece of cheese fell down. The fox ate it and said, "She hasn't got a beautiful voice and she hasn't got any brains."

译 文

1 乌鸦站在树上，嘴里叼着一大块奶酪。一只狐狸经过，看到了乌鸦和她的奶酪。他说："多么美的鸟呀！多么漂亮的眼睛啊！多么漂亮的羽毛呀！我很好奇她的声音也会很美妙吗！"乌鸦听到后便张开嘴唱："呱，呱。"这时，奶酪也跟着掉下来了。狐狸把它吃了，说："她的嗓音一点也不美，而且根本没有脑子。"

阅读无障碍

cheese [tʃiːz] *n.* 奶酪

beak [biːk] *n.* 鸟嘴

feather [ˈfeðə] *n.* 羽毛

wonder [ˈwʌndə(r)] *v.* 对……感到好奇

caw [kɔː] *v.* 发出鸦叫声

fall down 跌落

voice [vɔis] *n.* 嗓音

brain [breɪn] *n.* 头脑

The Wolf and the Lamb

狼和小羊

读一读，想一想

1. 小羊在哪里喝水？
2. 狼是怎样刁难小羊的？
3. 这个故事告诉了我们什么道理？

精彩故事欣赏

1 Once upon a time a wolf was lapping at a stream and saw a lamb drinking a little lower down. "This is my supper," he thought. "I will find some excuses to catch it." Then he shouted at the lamb, "How dare you foul the water?" "No, master," said the lamb. "I cannot foul your water because it runs down from you to me." "Well, then," said the wolf. "Why did you speak ill of me this time last year?" "It was impossible," said the lamb. "I am only six months old." "I don't care," shouted the wolf. "If it was not you, it must be your father." After that he rushed at the poor

译　文

1 从前，一只狼在小溪旁溜达，看到一只小羊在下游喝水。"这就是我的晚餐啦，"狼想，"我要找一个借口吃掉它。"于是，他朝小羊吼道："你怎么敢把我的水弄脏了！""我没有，先生，"小羊回答说，"我不可能弄脏你的水，因为我在你的下游啊。""那么，"狼又说道，"你去年的这时候为什么说我的坏话？""那不可能，"小羊说，"我现在只有六个

little lamb and ate it up.

月大。”“我不管，”狼大声吼，说，“就算不是你，那也肯定是你的爸爸。”说完后，他就冲向这只可怜的小羊，把它吃掉了。

stream [striːm] *n.* 小溪
excuse [ɪkˈskjuːzː] *n.* 借口
how dare you（表示震惊和愤怒）你竟敢
foul [faʊl] *v.* 弄脏
ill [ɪl] *n.* 坏话
impossible [ɪmˈpɒsɪb(ə)l] *adj.* 不可能的
rush [rʌʃ] *v.* 冲
poor [pɔː(r)] *adj.* 贫穷的

The Peacock and the Crane

孔雀与鹤

读一读，想一想

1. 孔雀为什么嘲笑鹤?
2. 鹤是怎么反驳孔雀的?
3. 这个故事告诉了我们什么道理?

精彩故事欣赏

1 A peacock was spreading his beautiful plumage, just then a crane passed by. The crane had grey feathers. The peacock looked at him and laughed, "I am robed in golden and purple. I look like a king. I'm also as splendid as the rainbow. But how about you? You have not any beautiful color on your wings." "True,"replied the crane." But I can fly very high, and lift up my voice to reach the stars while you can only walk like a cock."

译文

1 一只孔雀正展示他那美丽的翎羽，正在那时，一只鹤从旁边走过，鹤长了一身灰暗的羽毛，孔雀看了看，大笑了起来:“我穿着金色配紫色的长袍，看起来像个国王。我还像彩虹一样高贵艳丽，但是你呢？你的翅膀上连一点儿漂亮颜色也没有。”“确实。”鹤回答道。“可是我能飞上高空，我的声音能高达星辰，而你却只能像只公鸡一样走在地上。”

spread [spred] *v.* 伸展

plumage [ˈpluːmɪdʒ] *n.* 鸟类羽毛

robe [rəʊb] *v.* 使穿长袍

golden [ˈgəʊldən] *adj.* 金（黄）色的

king [kiŋ] *n.* 国王

splendid [ˈsplendɪd] *adj.* 灿烂的

rainbow [ˈreɪnbəʊ] *n.* 彩虹

cock [kɒk] *n.* 公鸡

The Cat And the Birds

猫和鸟

读一读，想一想

1. 猫为什么要假扮医生？
2. 鸟儿们相信猫吗？
3. 这个故事告诉我们什么道理？

精彩故事欣赏

1 A cat heard that the birds in an aviary were ailing, so he dressed himself up like a doctor. And taking his cane and the instruments to show his profession, he went to the aviary, knocked at the door, and said that if the birds were ill, he would be happy to prescribe for them and cure them. The birds replied, "If only you are good enough to go away, and leave us as we are, we will be all very well."

译文

1 有一只猫听说某个鸟舍里的鸟儿们都病了，便假扮成医生，为了显得专业，他带着手杖和医用工具，来到鸟舍前敲了敲门说，如果鸟儿们生病了，他愿意给他们开药医治。鸟儿们回答说："只要你发发善心离开这儿，让我们和以前一样住在这里，我们都会好起来的。"

阅读无障碍

aviary [ˈeɪvɪərɪ] *n.* 大型鸟舍
ailing [ˈeɪlɪŋ] *adj.* 生病的
dress [dres] *v.* 给……穿衣
cane [keɪn] *n.* 手杖
instrument [ˈɪnstrʊm(ə)nt] *n.* 器械
knock [nɒk] *v.* 敲击
prescribe [prɪˈskraɪb] *v.* 开药方
cure [kjʊəː] *v.* 治疗；治愈

The Moon and her Mother
月亮和妈妈

读一读，想一想

1. 月亮想向她的妈妈要什么东西？
2. 月亮的愿望最后实现了吗？为什么？

精彩故事欣赏

1 The moon once begged her mother to make a gown for her. "How can I?" replied she, "there's no gown fitting your figure. At one time you're a new moon, and at another you're a full moon, and between whiles you're neither one nor the other."

译 文

1 有一次，月亮乞求她的妈妈给她做一件长袍，"我怎么可能做呢？"妈妈回答道，"根本没有适合你体型的袍子。有时候你是新月，有时候是满月，而且你经常在两者之间变换。"

阅读无障碍

beg [beg] *v.* 乞讨；恳求

gown [gaʊn] *n.* 长袍

fit [fɪt] *v.* 使……合身

figure [ˈfɪgə] *n.*（人的）体形

full moon 满月

between [bɪˈtwiːn] *prep.* 在……之间

neither [ˈnaɪðə(r)] *conj.* 也不

The Ass, the Fox, and the Lion 驴子、狐狸和狮子

读一读，想一想

1. 狐狸为什么要陷害驴子？
2. 狮子最后有没有遵守诺言？
3. 这个故事告诉了我们什么道理？

精彩故事欣赏

1 The ass and the fox entered into a partnership together for their mutual protection and went into the forest to hunt. They had not proceeded far, when they met a lion. The fox, seeing the imminence of the danger, promised the lion to help him capture the ass, if only he would not injure him. The fox led the ass to a deep pit, and contrived him to fall into it. The lion seeing that the ass was in his possession, immediately clutched the fox, and then attacked the ass at his leisure.

译　文

1 驴子和狐狸结成联盟去林中打猎。他们走了没多远，就遇见一只狮子。狐狸见危险当前，便承诺狮子帮他抓住驴子，只要狮子不伤害自己。狮子答应了，狐狸就引驴子往一个深坑去，使它掉下陷阱。狮子看见驴子已经到手了，立刻先捉住狐狸，然后抽空吃掉了驴子。

partnership [ˈpɑːtnəʃɪp] *n.* 合伙
mutual [ˈmjuːtʃʊəl] *adj.* 共同的
protection [prəˈtekʃ(ə)n] *n.* 保护
proceed [prəˈsiːd] *v.* 继续进行
imminence [ˈɪmɪnəns] *n.* 危急
capture [ˈkæptʃə(r)] *n.* 危急
injure [ˈɪndʒə] *v.* 伤害

pit [pɪt] *n.* 深坑
contrive [kənˈtraɪv] *v.* 谋划
possession [pəˈzeʃ(ə)n] *n.* 拥有
clutch [klʌtʃ] *v.* 抓住
attack [əˈtæk] *v.* 攻击
leisure [ˈleʒə] *n.* 空闲

The Lion and the Mouse
狮子与报恩的老鼠

读一读，想一想

1. 狮子听到老鼠的话后为什么笑？
2. 你觉得老鼠真的很弱小吗？
3. 老鼠是怎样帮助狮子脱困的？

精彩故事欣赏

1 Once a lion was sleeping in a wood. A little mouse happened to come and ran over his face. The lion woke up and caught the little mouse in anger, and was going to kill her. " Oh, dear lion!" said the little mouse. " Please forgive me. I didn't mean to do you any harm. If you me go. I shall return your kindness."

2 "Ha, ha, ha," laughed the lion. "How can a little thing like you help a great lion?" He let her go then." Thank you very much, kind lion! I hope I shall be able to do you a good return some day," said the

译　文

1 从前，一只狮子在森林里睡觉，突然有一只小老鼠在他脸上跑过。狮子被惊醒了，生气地抓住了老鼠，打算吃掉她。“哦，亲爱的狮子大人，”小老鼠说，“请您原谅我，我并不想伤害您，如果您放了我，我会报答您的恩情的。”

2 “哈哈哈，”狮子笑着说，“你一只小小的老鼠怎么能帮助一只强壮的狮子呢？”然后就放走了他。“太

little mouse.

感谢你了，善良的狮子，我希望有一天能好好报答你。”小老鼠回答道。

3 Some time after this, the lion was caught in a trap. Just then the little mouse came along. At once she ran up to the lion and gnawed the ropes of the trap with her sharp teeth, and the lion was happy to be free again and say thanks to the little mouse.

3 在这以后的某一天，狮子落入了一个陷阱。正在那时，小老鼠经过，她立即跑到狮子面前，用她锋利的牙齿咬断了陷阱里的绳子。狮子很开心能重获自由并感谢了小老鼠。

阅读无障碍

wood [wʊd] *n.* 树林
anger [ˈæŋgə] *n.* 愤怒
forgive [fəˈgɪv] *v.* 原谅
harm [hɑːm] *n.* 伤害
return [rɪˈtɜːn] *v.* 返回
kindness [ˈkaɪn(d)nɪs] *n.* 仁慈
trap [træp] *n.* 陷阱
gnaw [nɔː] *v.* 咬
sharp [ʃɑːp] *adj.* 锋利的

The Crow and the Pitcher

乌鸦和水罐

读一读，想一想

1. 刚开始乌鸦为什么喝不到水？
2. 乌鸦想到了什么方法才喝到水？
3. 这个故事告诉了我们什么道理？

精彩故事欣赏

1 A crow felt very thirsty. He looked for water everywhere. Finally, he found a pitcher. However, there was not a lot of water in the pitcher. His beak could not reach it. He tried again and again, but still could not touch the water. When he was about to give up, an idea came into his mind. He took a pebble and dropped it into the pitcher. Then he took another and dropped it in. Gradually, the water rose, and the crow was able to drink the water happily.

译　文

1 一只乌鸦口渴了，到处找水喝。最后，他找到了一个大水罐。然而，水罐里并没有很多水，他的嘴够不到，他试了一次又一次，都没有成功。就在他想放弃的时候，突然想到了一个方法。乌鸦叼来了一块鹅卵石投到水罐里，接着又叼了另一块放进去。渐渐地，水面升高了。乌鸦高兴地喝到了水。

thirsty [ˈθɜːsti] *adj.* 口渴的

pitcher [ˈpɪtʃə] *n.* 大水罐

beak [biːk] *n.* 鸟嘴

touch [tʌtʃ] *v.* 触摸

pebble [ˈpeb(ə)l] *n.* 卵石

drop [drɒp] *v.* 扔

gradually [ˈgrædʒʊlɪ] *adv.* 渐渐地

rise [raɪz] *v.* 上升

The North Wind and the Sun 北风与太阳

读一读，想一想

1. 北风与太阳为什么打赌？
2. 最后谁赢了？
3. 这个故事告诉我们在为人处世方面应该怎样做？

精彩故事欣赏

1 The north wind and the sun disputed who was more powerful, and agreed that the one who could strip traveler's clothes was the victor.

2 The north wind first tried his power and blew with all his might, but the keener he blasts, the closer the traveler wrapped his cloak . At last, he gave up the hope of victory and called the sun to see what he could do.

3 The sun suddenly shone out with all his warmth. The traveler no sooner felt his genial rays, then he took off one garment after another, and at last undressed.

译 文

1 北风和太阳为谁更有威力而争论不休。它们一致同意，能让旅人脱下衣服的那个人就是胜利者。

2 北风首先一显身手，用尽全力刮了起来，但是它刮得越猛烈，旅人把斗篷裹得越紧。最后他只能放弃获胜的希望，把太阳叫过来看看他能干什么。

3 于是，太阳突然释放出它全部的温暖。旅人立马就感受到了它亲切的光芒，

4 "I think that proves who is stronger." said the sun. But the north wind had crept away to hide.

然后一件一件地脱掉外面的衣服，最后终于脱光了。

4 太阳说："我想，这足以证明谁更强大了吧。"此时，风早已蹑手蹑脚地溜走，藏了起来。

阅读无障碍

dispute [dɪˈspjuːt] *v.* 辩论
strip [strɪp] *v.* 脱去衣服
victor [ˈvɪktə] *n.* 胜利者
blow [bləʊ] *v.* 风吹
might [maɪt] *n.* 力量
keen [kiːn] *adj.* 强烈的
blast [blɑːst] *v.* 猛吹
cloak [kləʊk] *n.* 斗篷
victory [ˈvɪkt(ə)rɪ] *n.* 胜利
shine [ʃaɪn] *v.* 发出光
warmth [wɔːmθ] *n.* 温暖
genial [ˈdʒiːnɪəl] *adj.* 亲切的
ray [reɪ] *n.* 光线
garment [ˈgɑːm(ə)nt] *n.* 衣服
undress [ʌnˈdres] *v.* 使脱衣服
prove [pruːv] *v.* 证明
creep [kriːp] *v.* 慢慢地移动

The Hares and the Frogs

野兔与青蛙

读一读，想一想

1. 野兔们为什么要淹死自己?
2. 谁让野兔改变了想法?
3. 从这个故事中你学到了什么道理呢?

精彩故事欣赏

1 The hares complained about their unhappiness. They were in great danger for lacking strength and courage. Men, dogs, birds and beasts were all their enemies. They caught them and killed and then ate them. They lost their confidence and decided to end their lives. They rushed to a neighboring pool, intending to drown themselves. There were a number of frogs hiding themselves on the bank, after hearing the noise, they were frightened in their turn by the approach of the hares and leaped into the water. Then one of

译 文

1 野兔们抱怨他们活得不快乐。因为缺乏力量和勇气，他们总是处于危险之中。人类，狗，鸟还有野兽都是他们的敌人一直抓他们然后吃掉。野兔们失去了信心，想结束生命。他们冲到了附近的一个水池，打算淹死自己。有一群青蛙藏在岸边，在听到吵闹声后，他们害怕野兔们靠近就跳进了水里。这时，一只聪明年长的

the older, wise hares cried out, “stop, my friends, do not let us destroy ourselves. There are more creatures who are afraid of us, and also must be still more timid than ourselves.”

野兔喊道：“我的朋友们，快停下来，我们不能自己毁了自己。世上还有害怕我们的动物呢，他们肯定比我们更胆小！”

阅读无障碍

complain [kəm'pleɪn] *v.* 抱怨

unhappiness [ʌn'hæpinis] *n.* 苦恼

lack [læk] *v.* 缺乏

strength [streŋθ] *n.* 力量

courage ['kʌrɪdʒ] *n.* 勇气

enemy ['enəmɪ] *n.* 敌人

confidence ['kɒnfɪd(ə)ns] *n.* 信心

rush [rʌʃ] *v.* 冲

intend [ɪn'tend] *v.* 打算；想要

frightened ['fraɪtnd] *adj.* 害怕的；受惊的

leap [li:p] *v.* 跳跃

destroy [dɪ'strɒɪ] *v.* 破坏；消灭

creature ['kri:tʃə] *n.* 动物，生物

timid ['tɪmɪd] *adj.* 胆小的；羞怯的

The Fox and the Stork

狐狸与鹳

读一读，想一想

1. 狐狸为什么用浅盘子盛汤？
2. 鹳是怎么报复狐狸的？
3. 这个故事告诉了我们怎样的道理？

精彩故事欣赏

1 Once a fox invited a stork to have a dinner . He put nothing on the table except some soup in a very shallow dish. The fox could easily drink the soup, but the stork could only wet the end of her long bill. When she left the meal, she was still very hungry. "I am sorry," said the fox, "the soup doesn't suit your taste." "Please do not apologize," said the stork. "I hope you can have a dinner with me in my house in a few days later." However, when the fox visited the stork, he found that his food was in a long bottle with a narrow mouth.

译 文

1 从前，一只狐狸请鹳来吃饭。他只用一个浅浅的盘子盛了一点汤。狐狸可以轻而易举地喝到汤，但是鹳只能蘸湿他长长的嘴尖。吃完饭后，鹳仍然很饿。“很抱歉，”狐狸说，“这汤不合你的口味。”“不用道歉，”鹳说，“我希望几天后你能到我家和我一起吃顿饭。”然而，当狐狸到鹳家做客时，他发现自己的食物在一个细

He could not put his big mouth into it, so he ate nothing. "I will not apologize," said the stork. "One bad turn deserves another."

口的瓶子里，他无法将他的嘴伸进去，所以什么也吃不到。"我不会道歉的，"鹳说，"这叫一报还一报。"

except [ɪkˈsept] *prep.* 除……之外
shallow [ˈʃæləʊ] *adj.* 浅的
bill [bɪl] *n.* 喙
suit [suːt] *v.* 适合
taste [teɪst] *n.* 口味
apologize [əˈpɒlədʒaɪz] *v.* 道歉
narrow [ˈnærəʊ] *adj.* 狭窄的
deserve [dɪˈzɜːv] *v.* 应受

The Wolf in Sheep's Clothing

披着羊皮的狼

读一读，想一想

1. 狼刚开始为什么不敢吃羊？
2. 狼想了什么办法混入羊群？
3. 小羊为什么跟着狼出了羊群？

精彩故事欣赏

1 A wolf wanted to eat the sheep, but he was afraid of the vigilant shepherd and his dogs. One day the wolf found the skin of a sheep. He put it on and walked among the sheep. A lamb thought that the wolf was its mother because his skin looked like hers. So it followed the wolf. Soon after they had left the dogs, the wolf caught the lamb and ate it up. For some time he succeeded in deceiving the sheep, and enjoying hearty meals.

译　文

1 一只狼想吃羊，但是他害怕警惕的牧羊人和牧羊犬。有一天这只狼发现了一块羊皮，便披着它混入羊群。一只小羊羔把这只披着羊皮的狼误认为自己的妈妈。所以他跟着狼出了羊群，很快便甩掉了牧羊犬。狼就把小羊羔抓住吃掉了。此后，他便成功的欺骗了羊群，并且享受美味的大餐了。

阅读无障碍

vigilant [ˈvɪdʒɪl(ə)nt] *adj.* 警惕的
shepherd [ˈʃepəd] *n.* 牧羊人
skin [skɪn] *n.* 外皮
follow [ˈfɒləʊ] *v.* 跟随
succeed [səkˈsiːd] *v.* 成功
deceive [dɪˈsiːv] *v.* 欺诈
hearty [ˈhɑːtɪ] *adj.* 丰盛的
meal [miːl] *n.* 餐

The Stag in the Ox-Stall
牛棚里的雄鹿

读一读，想一想

1. 雄鹿跑到什么地方躲避猎狗？
2. 猎人们发现雄鹿了吗？为什么？
3. 最后雄鹿被谁发现了？为什么？

精彩故事欣赏

1 A stag was being pursued by some dogs. It ran into an ox-stall, and hid itself in a mound of hay. Only the tips of its horns could be seen. In no time the hunters came there, and asked if anyone had seen the stag. The cowboys said they saw nothing. So the hunters went away. Later the master came in. He looked around and saw something unusual. He pointed at the mound of hay and asked, "What are those two strange things?" When the cowboys went to check, they discovered the stag.

译　文

1 一只雄鹿被猎狗追赶，于是跑进了一个牛栏里，躲在一大堆干草里面，只有鹿角尖露在外面。猎人们很快就追到了这里，询问是否有人看到这头鹿。牛仔们说他们什么也没有看到，于是猎人们走了。不久，主人回来了，他四处查看时，看到了异常的东西。他指着那堆干草问："那两个怪模怪样的东西是什么？"牛仔们检查的时候发现了这只鹿。

阅读无障碍

pursue [pəˈsjuː] *v.* 追赶

mound [maʊnd] *n.* 堆

tip [tɪp] *n.* 尖端

horn [hɔːn] *n.* 角

unusual [ʌnˈjuːʒʊəl] *adj.* 不寻常的

strange [streɪn(d)ʒ] *adj.* 奇怪的

check [tʃek] *v.* 检查

discover [dɪˈskʌvə] *v.* 发现

The Dolphins, the Whales, and the Sprat

海豚、鲸和西鲱鱼

读一读，想一想

1. 谁在打架？
2. 西鲱鱼打算怎么做？他成功了吗？
3. 这个故事给你什么启发？

精彩故事欣赏

1 The dolphins argued with the whales, they have been fighting with one another for a long time. And there is no sign of end to this fierce battle. When a sprat thought that perhaps he could stop it. So he prepared to persuade them to give up fighting and make friends. But one of the dolphins said to him contemptuously, "We would rather keep fighting until we're all killed than be compromised by a sprat like you!"

译 文

1 海豚与鲸争辩，他们彼此斗争了好久，而且没有要停的迹象。有一条西鲱鱼认为自己或许能够阻止他们的战争，便准备劝他们放弃争斗，成为朋友。但是其中一只海豚轻蔑地对他说："我们宁可打到同归于尽，也不会因为一条像你这样的西鲱鱼而和解。"

阅读无障碍

sign [saɪn] *n.* 迹象

fierce [fɪəs] *adj.* 猛烈的

battle [ˈbæt(ə)l] *n.* 斗争

prepare [prɪˈpeə] *v.* 准备

persuade [pəˈsweɪd] *v.* 劝说

contemptuously [kənˈtemptjuəsli] *adv.* 轻蔑地

rather [ˈrɑːðə(r)] *adv.* 宁愿

cmpromise [ˈkɒmprəmaɪz] *v.* 和解

The Fox and the Monkey

狐狸和猴子

读一读，想一想

1. 狐狸和猴子在路上看到了什么？
2. 狐狸同意猴子的话吗？

精彩故事欣赏

1 A fox and a monkey were traveling together on the same road. As they walked, they passed through a graveyard full of monuments. "All these monuments which you see," said the monkey, pointing to those monuments, "are erected in honor of my ancestors, who were in their day freedmen and citizens of great fame." The fox replied, "You have chosen a most appropriate subject for your lie and I am sure none of them will be able to contradict you."

译　文

1 狐狸与猴子在同一条路上旅行。他们路过了一个满是墓碑的墓地。这时，猴子指着那些墓碑说："你在这里看到的所有墓碑都是我祖先的荣誉，他们在那个年代都是很有名望的人！"狐狸回答道："你为你的谎言选择了一个很恰当的话题，我相信他们之中没有人能站起来反驳你。"

阅读无障碍

monument [ˈmɒnjʊm(ə)nt] *n.* 纪念碑

erect [ɪˈrekt] *v.* 使竖立

honor [ˈɒnə(r)] *n.* 荣誉

ancestor [ˈænsestə] *n.* 祖先

freedman [ˈfriːdmən] *n.* 自由民

citizen [ˈsitizən] *n.* 公民

fame [feɪm] *n.* 名望

appropriate [əˈprəʊprɪət] *adj.* 适当的

subject [ˈsʌbdʒekt] *n.* 主题

lie [laɪ] *n.* 谎言

contradict [kɒntrəˈdɪkt] *v.* 反驳

The Ass and the Lap-Dog

驴和哈巴狗

读一读，想一想

1. 主人最喜欢的家畜是谁？
2. 哈巴狗是怎样讨好主人的？
3. 驴子最后的下场是什么？

精彩故事欣赏

1 One day a farmer came to the stables to see his beasts, among them was his favorite donkey which was always fed well and often carried his master. The lapdog came with the farmer, he danced about and licked his hand and frisked about as happy as he could. The farmer was pleased and gave the lapdog some dainty food as reward. He jumped into his master's lap, and lay there blinking while the farmer stroked his ears.

2 The donkey, seeing this, began to

译 文

1 一天，农夫去马厩里看他的牲畜，其中他最喜欢的就是驴，这头驴被饲养的很好，常被当作主人的坐骑。一只哈巴狗也随着主人活蹦乱跳的来到马厩，时而作揖，时而跳跃，极尽能事。主人把精美的食物奖励给了他。他就跳到农夫的膝盖上，眼睛一眨一眨的，农夫高兴地抚摸着它的耳朵。

2 驴看到了这情景，开

imitate the dog to prance. The farmer could not help laughing .So the donkey went up to him, and put his feet upon the farmer's shoulder in order to climb into his lap. The farmer's servants rushed up with sticks and pitchforks and soon taught the donkey that clumsy jesting is no joke.

始模仿哈巴狗蹦跶起来，农夫看了禁不住哈哈大笑。看到这个情形，驴便走向农夫，将双蹄搭向农夫的肩膀，也想坐到农夫的膝盖上。周围的仆人马上冲过来，用棍棒和干草叉教会了驴，开这种不合时宜的玩笑可不是闹着玩的。

阅读无障碍

stable [ˈsteɪb(ə)l] *n.* 马厩
beast [biːst] *n.* 畜生
feed [fiːd] *v.* 喂养
carry [ˈkærɪ] *v.* 运载
lick [lɪk] *v.* 舔
frisk [frɪsk] *v.* 蹦跳
dainty [ˈdeɪntɪ] *adj.* 美味的
reward [rɪˈwɔːd] *v.* 眨眼
lay [leɪ] *v.* 躺下
blink [blɪŋk] *v.* 眨眼
stroke [strəʊk] *v.* 轻抚
imitate [ˈɪmɪteɪt] *v.* 模仿
prance [prɑːns] *v.* 腾跃
shoulder [ˈʃəʊldə] *n.* 肩
servant [ˈsɜːv(ə)nt] *n.* 仆人
rush [rʌʃ] *v.* 冲
stick [stɪk] *n.* 棍
pitchfork [ˈpɪtʃfɔːk] *n.* 干草叉
clumsy [ˈklʌmzɪ] *adj.* 不得当的
jesting [ˈdʒestiŋ] *n.* 笑话

The Fir-Tree and the Bramble 冷杉与荆棘

读一读，想一想

1. 这个故事告诉了我们什么道理？
2. 你觉得冷杉比荆棘更有用处吗？

精彩故事欣赏

1 A fir-tree was boasting to a bramble, and said contemptuously, "You are a poor and useless creature. Now, look at me: I am useful for the things, particularly when men build houses, they can't do anything without me." But the bramble replied, "Ah, that's right. But when they come with axes and saws to cut you down, and then you'll wish you were a bramble and not a fir."

译 文

1 一棵冷杉树用轻蔑的口吻对着荆棘炫耀道："你是个又可怜又没用的东西，你现在看看我，我可是对所有东西都有用处，尤其是当人类要盖房子的时候，没有我根本就不行。"但是荆棘回答："是啊！你说得对，不过，等他们拿着斧头来把你砍倒的时候，你就会希望自己是一棵荆棘，而不是冷杉树了。"

阅读无障碍

boast [bəʊst] *v.* 夸口说

contemptuously [kənˈtemptjuəsli] *adv.* 轻蔑地

useless [ˈjuːsləs] *adj.* 无用的

creature [ˈkriːtʃə(r)] *n.* 生物

useful [ˈjuːsfl] *adj.* 有用的

particularly [pəˈtɪkjʊləlɪ] *adv.* 特别地

axe [æks] *n.* 斧

saw [sɔː] *n.* 锯子

The Frogs' Complaint Against the Sun

抱怨太阳的青蛙

读一读，想一想

1. 青蛙们为什么很惊恐？
2. 这个故事给你什么启发？

精彩故事欣赏

1 Once upon a time the sun was about to find a wife for himself. After knowing this, the frogs all raised their voices to the skies in terror. Jupiter, who was disturbed by the noise, asked them what they were croaking about. They replied, "The sun is bad enough to dry up our marshes with his heat when he is single. But what shall we do if he marries and begets other suns?"

译文

1 从前，太阳想给自己找个老婆。知道这个消息后，青蛙们惊恐地冲着天空大喊，朱庇特被吵闹声扰的心烦意乱，就问他们在哇哇乱叫什么。他们回答说："即便是单身，太阳已经够坏了，几乎晒干了我们的沼泽地，要是他再结了婚，并且再有了别的小太阳的话，我们该怎么办呀？"

阅读无障碍

raise [reɪz] *v.* 提高

terror [ˈterə] *n.* 恐惧

disturb [dɪˈstɜːb] *v.* 打扰

croak [krəʊk] *v.* 呱呱地叫

marsh [mɑːʃ] *n.* 沼泽；

single [ˈsɪŋg(ə)l] *adj.* 单身的

marry [ˈmæri] *v.*（使）结婚

beget [bɪˈget] *v.* 当……的父亲

The Dog, the Cock, and the Fox 狗、公鸡和狐狸

读一读，想一想

1. 公鸡晚上怎样睡觉？
2. 狐狸为什么乞求公鸡下来？
3. 这个故事告诉了我们什么道理？

精彩故事欣赏

1 A dog and a cock became good friends, and determined to travel together. At night the cock flied into a tree to sleep, while the dog slept inside the empty trunk. When the day is coming, the cock woke up and crew as usual. A fox heard wanted to eat the cock, so he came and stood under the tree and begged the cock to come down. He said, "I am happy to meet you, because your voice is nice." The cock replied, "Would you just wake my friend? He sleeps at the foot of the tree. He'll open the door and let you in." The fox did it, the dog came out and killed the fox.

译　文

1 一只狗与一只公鸡成了好朋友，他们决定一起去旅行。晚上，公鸡跳到树枝上睡觉，而狗则在下面的树洞里过夜。天快亮时，公鸡像往常一样打起了鸣，一只狐狸听到鸡叫，就想把他吃掉，便跑来站在树下，乞求公鸡下来。他说，“我很高兴能认识你，因为你声音太好听了。”公鸡回答说：“你能先叫醒我的朋友吗？他在树洞里睡觉。他会给你打开

门让你进来的。”狐狸照做了，结果狗跑出来把他咬死了。

阅读无障碍

determine [dɪˈtɜːmɪn] *v.* 决定，确定
travel [ˈtrævl] *v.* 旅行
inside [ˌɪnˈsaɪd] *prep.* 在……以内
empty [ˈempti] *adj.* 空的

trunk [trʌŋk] *n.* 树干；躯干
as usual 像往常一样
beg [beg] *v.* 恳求
wake [weɪk] *v.* 叫醒

The Gnat and the Bull

蠓虫和公牛

读一读，想一想

1. 公牛会想念蠓虫吗？
2. 这个故事给了我们什么启示？

精彩故事欣赏

1 A gnat settled on the horn of a bull for a long time. When he was going to leave, he made some buzz, and asked the bull if he would miss him. The bull replied, "I did not know when you came, and I shall not miss you when you go away."

译　文

1 有只蠓虫落到一只公牛的角上，停留了好久。当他要走的时候，发出了一阵嗡嗡声，问公牛是否会想念他。公牛回答说："我都不知道你什么时候来的，你走的时候又怎么会想念你呢。"

阅读无障碍

settle [ˈset(ə)l] v.（鸟、昆虫）降落
horn [hɔːn] n. 角
leave [liːv] v. 离开
buzz [bʌz] n. 嗡嗡声
miss [mɪs] v. 思念
go away 离开

The Oak and the Reeds

橡树与芦苇

读一读，想一想

1. 橡树为什么落到了河对面？
2. 芦苇为什么能承受住强风？
3. 你从这个故事里能学到什么？

精彩故事欣赏

1 On the bank of a river, there was an oak. One day, it was uprooted by a strong wind, and then it was thrown across the river. It fell into some reeds, which are growing by the water. The oak said to them, "I don't understand why you can stand the strong wind, since you are so frail, and why I can be uprooted, since I am so strong?" The reeds replied, "You were so stubborn, and fought against the storm which are stronger than you. But we bow and yield to every breeze, so the wind passed over our heads and won't hurt us."

译文

1 从前有一颗橡树生长在河岸上，一天，它被一阵强风连根拔起，扔到了河对面。他落到了在水边生长的一堆芦苇中，于是他对芦苇说："我很不理解，为什么你们如此脆弱，却能承受住强风，而我这么强壮，都能被狂风连根拔起呢？"芦苇回答道："你太顽固了，总是喜欢和比你强壮的风对抗。但是我们对微风都卑躬屈膝，

所以强风吹过我们的头顶，
却不会伤害我们。”

阅读无障碍

uprooted [ʌpˈruːt] *v.* 连根拔起
throw [θrəʊ] *v.* 抛
frail [freɪl] *adj.* 脆弱的
stubborn [ˈstʌbən] *adj.* 顽固的
fight against 与……作斗争
bow [baʊ] *v.* 鞠躬
yield [jiːld] *v.* 屈服
breeze [briːz] *n.* 微风

The Wolf and the Crane

狼与鹤

读一读，想一想

1. 狼为什么雇佣鹤？
2. 鹤是怎样把骨头拔出来的？
3. 狼给鹤报酬了吗？

精彩故事欣赏

1 A wolf who had a bone stuck in his throat hired a crane, for a large sum, to put her head into his mouth and draw out the bone. When the crane had extracted the bone and demanded the promised payment, the wolf, grinning and grinding his teeth, exclaimed: "Why, you have surely already had a sufficient recompense, in having been permitted to draw out your head in safety from the mouth and jaws of a wolf."

译 文

1 一只狼误吞下了一块骨头，卡在嗓子里十分难受。于是他重金雇佣鹤，让他把头伸进自己的嘴巴里帮自己取出骨头。商定好了以后，鹤于是按照要求拔出了骨头，然后便向狼要定好的酬金。狼却说道："什么？还跟我要报酬！你能把头从狼嘴里平安无事地收回来，难道这不算充足的报酬吗？"

hire [ˈhaɪə(r)] *v.* 雇用

sum [sʌm] *n.* 金额

extract [ˈekstrækt] *v.* 拔出

demand [dɪˈmɑːnd] *v.* 要求

grin [grɪn] *v.* 露齿而笑

grind [graɪnd] *v.* 磨

sufficient [səˈfɪʃnt] *adj.* 足够的

recompense [ˈrekəmpens] *n.* 报酬

The Fox and the Goat
狐狸和山羊

读一读，想一想

1. 山羊为什么跳进了井里？
2. 狐狸是怎样跳出井的？

精彩故事欣赏

1 An unlucky fox fell into a well. The well is so deep and the fox can't go out of it. A goat passed by and asked the fox what he was doing in the well. "Oh, didn't you hear that?" said the fox. "There is going to be a dry weather, so I jumped down to get some water. Why don't you come down here too?" The goat believed his words, and jumped down into the well. But the fox quickly jumped on the goat's back and jumped out of the well. "Goodbye, friend," said the fox. "Remember next time don't believe the advice of a man in difficulties."

译　文

1 一只倒霉的狐狸掉到了一口井里。井很深，他没有办法跳出来。一只山羊经过这里，便问狐狸在井下做什么。狐狸说："哦，你没有听说吗？这里将要大旱，因此我跳进来取水，为什么你不下来和我一起呢？"山羊相信了狐狸的话，也跳进了井里。但是狐狸立即跳上山羊的背，跳出了井。"再见，朋友，"狐狸说，"记住，不要相信一个身陷麻烦的人的建议。"

well [wel] *n.* 井；源泉

deep [diːp] *adj.* 深的

pass by 经过

dry [draɪ] *adj.* 干的

weather [ˈweðə(r)] *n.* 天气

believe [bɪˈliːv] *v.* 相信

advice [ədˈvaɪs] *n.* 建议

difficulty [ˈdɪfɪk(ə)ltɪ] *n.* 困境

The Crab and his Mother

小螃蟹和他的妈妈

读一读，想一想

1. 螃蟹横着走还是竖着走呢？
2. 小螃蟹同意妈妈说的话吗？
3. 你觉得小螃蟹说的对吗？

精彩故事欣赏

1 A crab said to her son, "Why do you walk sideways, my child? Go straight forward." The young crab replied: "Quite right, dear mother, and if you will show me the straight way, I will promise to walk as you told me." The mother tried in vain, and had nothing more to say for her son's blame.

译 文

1 一只螃蟹对她的儿子说："我的孩子，为什么横着走呢？要直着往前走！"小螃蟹回答说："妈妈，您说得完全正确。如果您给我示范一下怎样直着走，我就答应按照您说的做。"螃蟹妈妈试了试，可只是徒劳无功，她对儿子的责备没话可说了。

阅读无障碍

sideways [ˈsaɪdweɪz] *adv.* 斜着
straight [streɪt] *adv.* 直接地
forward [ˈfɔːwəd] *adv.* 向前地
quite [kwaɪt] *adv.* 相当
promise [ˈprɒmɪs] *v.* 允诺，许诺
in vain 徒劳无益地
blame [bleɪm] *n.* 责备

The Ass and his Shadow

驴和他的影子

读一读，想一想

1. 旅人和驴子的主任为什么争吵?
2. 他们俩的争吵有结果吗?
3. 这个故事告诉了我们什么道理?

1 A traveler hired an ass to carry him to the distance. That weather is very hot, and the sun shining in its strength, the traveler stopped to have a rest, and sought shelter under the shadow of the ass. As this afforded protection for only one person, the traveler and the owner of the ass started a violent dispute about which of them had the right to it . The owner maintained that he had let the ass himself, and not his shadow. The traveler asserted that he employed both the ass and his shadow. The quarrel proceeded from words to blows, and while the men fought, the ass ran away.

1 一个旅人雇用了一只驴子载他去远方。天气很炎热，太阳曝晒，旅人便停下来休息，在驴子的影子下乘凉。由于影子只能遮住一个人，而旅人和驴子的主人两人便激烈的争吵了起来，争论他们当中哪一个人有权利在驴的影子下乘凉。驴子的主人坚持说他只出租驴子本身，不包括驴子的影子。旅人则宣称，他把驴和影子一起雇用了。他们争吵不休，

从叫骂发展到了互殴，而就在他们打架时，驴子却逃跑了。

阅读无障碍

hire [ˈhaɪə] *v.* 雇用
distance [ˈdɪst(ə)ns] *n.* 远方
strength [streŋθ] *n.* 力量
seek [siːk] *v.* 寻找
afford [əˈfɔːd] *v.* 提供
protection [prəˈtekʃ(ə)n] *n.* 保护
violent [ˈvaɪəl(ə)nt] *adj.* 暴力的
dispute [dɪˈspjuːt;] *n.* 争吵
maintain [meɪnˈteɪn] *v.* 主张
assert [əˈsɜːt] *v.* 声称
employ [ɪmˈplɒɪ] *v.* 雇用
quarrel [ˈkwɒr(ə)l] *n.* 吵架
proceed [prəˈsiːd] *v.* 继续进行
blow [bləʊ] *n.* 殴打

The Monkey as King
当上国王的猴子

读一读，想一想

1. 猴子是怎样成为国王的？
2. 猴子为什么跑到了捕兽夹上？
3. 从这个故事你能学到什么？

精彩故事欣赏

1 A monkey once danced in an assembly of the beasts, and so pleased them. So they elected him their king. A fox was very jealous of his honor. When he discovered a piece of meat lying in a trap, he led the monkey to it and said that she had found a treasure and decided to keep it for the monkey his kingdom. The careless monkey approached in excitement and was caught in the trap, and on his accusing the fox of purposely leading him into the snare, she replied, " Monkey, with such a mind as yours, are you going to be king over the beasts?"

译 文

1 有一次，猴子在野兽的集会上跳舞，赢得了大家的好感，他们选举他为国王。一只狐狸很嫉妒他。当他发现有一片肉放在捕兽夹上的时候，便把猴子领到那里去，说他发现一个宝物，并决定把它留给猴子和他的王国。粗心大意的猴子兴奋地跑了上去，结果被夹子夹住了。他指责狐狸陷害他，狐狸回答道："猴子，就凭你这个笨蛋脑袋还想做万兽之王吗？"

阅读无障碍

assembly [ə'semblɪ] *n.* 集会
beast [bi:st] *n.* 野兽
please [pli:z] *v.* 使喜欢
elect [ɪ'lekt] *v.* 选举
jealous ['dʒeləs] *adj.* 妒忌的
honor ['ɒnə(r)] *n.* 荣誉
discover [dɪ'skʌvə] *v.* 发现
trap [træp] *n.* 陷阱
treasure ['treʒə] *n.* 财富
kingdom ['kɪŋdəm] *n.* 王国
careless ['keələs] *adj.* 粗心的
approach [ə'prəʊtʃ] *v.* 接近
excitement [ɪk'saɪtmənt] *n.* 兴奋
accuse [ə'kju:z] *v.* 控告
purposely ['pɜ:pəslɪ] *adv.* 故意地
snare [sneə] *n.* 圈套

The Lamp
油灯

1. 油灯为什么夸口自己比太阳还亮？
2. 油灯被什么吹灭了？
3. 从人说的话中你能体会到什么？

精彩故事欣赏

1 A lamp which was filled with oil, burned with a clear and steady light, and began to boast that it shone more brightly than the sun. Just then a gust of wind blew it out. Someone struck a match and lit it again, and said, "You just keep alight, and never think of the sun. Because even the stars never need to be relit as you ."

译 文

1 有一盏装满油的油灯，在燃烧时发出了清晰稳定的亮光。油灯开始夸口说自己发出的光比太阳还要亮得多。就在这时，一阵风把灯给吹灭了，有人划了一根火柴并且重新点燃了它。并说道："你就好好亮着吧，永远不要去想太阳。因为即便是星星，也不会像你刚才一样需要重新被点燃。"

阅读无障碍

burn [bɜːn] *v.* 燃烧

steady [ˈstedɪ] *adj.* 稳定的

shine [ʃaɪn] *v.* 发出光

brightly [ˈbraɪtlɪ] *adv.* 明亮地

gust [gʌst] *n.* 一阵狂风

light [laɪt] *v.* 点着

alight [əˈlaɪt] *adj.* 烧着的

relight [ˈriːˈlaɪt] *v.* 重新燃点

The Owl and the Birds

猫头鹰和百鸟

读一读，想一想

1. 这个故事告诉了我们一个什么道理？

2. 如果现实生活中也有人像猫头鹰一样给你建议，你会怎么做呢？

精彩故事欣赏

1 An owl, in her wisdom, counseled the birds that when the acorn first began to sprout, to pull it all up out of the ground and not allow it to grow. She said acorns would produce mistletoe, from which an irremediable poison, the bird — lime, would be extracted and by which they would be captured. The owl next advised them to pluck up the seed of the flax, which men had sown, as it was a plant which boded no good to them. And, lastly, the owl, seeing an archer approach, predicted that this man, being on foot, would contrive darts armed with feathers which

译 文

1 智慧的猫头鹰劝告百鸟，橡树开始发芽时就要把橡树的芽苗拔了，不要让它生长。她说橡树会长出槲寄生，从中可以提炼出一种无法补救的毒药——黏鸟胶，而黏鸟胶可以捕捉鸟儿。猫头鹰接着又建议鸟儿们拔了人类播种的亚麻种子，因为这种植物对鸟儿们不利。最后，猫头鹰看到一个弓箭手靠近，她预言这个靠近的人会设计比鸟儿飞的还快的羽

would fly faster than the wings of the birds themselves. The birds gave no credence to these warning words, but considered the owl to be beside herself and said that she was mad. But afterwards, finding her words were true, they wondered at her knowledge and deemed her to be the wisest of birds. Hence it is that when she appears they look to her as knowing all things, while she no longer gives them advice, but in solitude laments their past folly.

毛箭。但是，百鸟们不但不信它的话，反而还认为她是个忘形的疯子。然而后来，百鸟们发现事实正如猫头鹰预言的那样，它们惊异于猫头鹰的智慧，并且视猫头鹰为最聪明的鸟类。此后，只要猫头鹰一出现，鸟儿们就会趋之若鹜，仿佛她无所不知，但猫头鹰不再提出忠告，而只是独自悲叹百鸟们以往的愚蠢。

阅读无障碍

counsel [ˈkaʊns(ə)l] *v.* 建议

sprout [sprəʊt] *v.* 发芽

mistletoe [ˈmɪs(ə)ltəʊ] *n.* 槲寄生（一种常用作圣诞节室内悬挂的植物）

irremediable [ɪrɪˈmiːdɪəb(ə)l] *adj.* 不能补救的

extract [ˈekstrækt] *v.* 提取

capture [ˈkæptʃə] *v.* 捕捉

pluck up 拔起

approach [əˈprəʊtʃ] *v.* 接近

predict [prɪˈdɪkt] *v.* 预言

give credence to 相信……

in solitude 独自

lament [ləˈment] *v.* 悲叹

The Ass in the Lion's Skin

披着狮皮的驴

读一读，想一想

1. 这个故事告诉了我们一个什么道理？
2. 以貌取人有哪些坏处？

精彩故事欣赏

1 An ass once found a lion's skin. He put it on, and walked towards the village.

2 All fled when he came near, both men and animals.

3 The ass felt quite proud. He lifted his voice and brayed, but then everyone knew him.

4 His owner came up and gave him a sound whipping.

5 Shortly afterwards, a fox came up to him and said, "Ah, I knew it was you by your voice."

译　文

1 有头驴捡到了一张狮子皮，他披上狮子皮往村庄走去。

2 所有的人和动物见到他走近都逃走了。

3 驴感到很得意，他大声嘶叫起来，但这一叫却被所有人认了出来。

4 他的主人跑过来给他好一顿鞭打。

5 没过多久，一只狐狸跑过来，对他说："哎，你一张嘴我就认出你来了。"

阅读无障碍

ass [æs] *n.* 驴子

put on 穿上

flee [fli:] *v.* 逃走

proud [praʊd] *adj.* 得意的

bray [breɪ] *v.* 叫

come up 走上前来

sound [saʊnd] *adj.* 充分的

whip [wɪp] *v.* 抽打

The She-Goats and Their Beards

母山羊和她们的胡须

读一读，想一想

1. 从这个故事当中，你可以悟出什么样的道理？
2. 外在的东西重要吗？你怎么看？

精彩故事欣赏

1 The she-goats having obtained by request from Jupiter the favor of a beard, the he-goats, sorely displeased, made complaint that the females equaled them in dignity. "Allow them," said Jupiter, "to enjoy an empty honor, and to assume the badge of your nobler sex, so long as they are not your equals in strength or courage."

2 It matters little if those who are inferior to us in merit should be like us in outside appearances.

译 文

1 母山羊请求并从宙斯天神那里得到了赏赐的胡须，公山羊很不高兴，向宙斯天神抱怨，说母山羊就要和它们一样尊贵了。天神说："允许她们享受一个虚空的荣誉吧，让她们也拥有如你们雄性一样的高贵，即便如此她们的力量和勇气却无法与你们匹敌！"

2 那些自身价值达不到我们的人，即便外貌跟我们相似也无关紧要。

阅读无障碍

obtain [əbˈteɪn] *v.* 获得

displease [dɪsˈpliːz] *v.* 使生气

make complaint 抱怨

equal in 在……方面相等

dignity [ˈdɪgnɪtɪ] *n.* 高贵

badge [bædʒ] *n.* 标记

strength [streŋθ] *n.* 力量

courage [ˈkʌrɪdʒ] *n.* 勇气

inferior [ɪnˈfɪərɪə] *adj.* 差的

The Old Lion

老狮子

读一读，想一想

1. 这个故事告诉了我们一个什么道理？
2. 老狮子为什么说自己死不瞑目？
3. 驴子的行为值得赞许吗？

精彩故事欣赏

1 A lion, worn out with years and powerless from disease, lay on the ground at the point of death. A boar rushed upon him, and avenged with a stroke of his tusks a long-remembered injury. Shortly afterwards the bull with his horns gored him as if he were an enemy. When the ass saw that the huge beast could be assailed with impunity, he let drive at his forehead with his heels. The expiring lion said, "I have reluctantly brooked the insults of the brave, but to be compelled to endure such treatment from thee, a disgrace to nature, is indeed to die a double death."

译 文

1 一头年久积劳疾病缠身的狮子，临死之际躺在地上。一头野猪冲到他身上，龇起獠牙攻击狮子以报它耿耿于怀的伤痛之仇。没过多久，一头公牛用他的尖角刺向狮子，仿佛狮子是他的仇敌。一头驴看到野猪跟公牛可以恣意妄为的攻击这头庞大的野兽时，于是便用自己的后脚去踢狮子的前额。这头快要断气的狮子说："我已勉强忍受了勇者的欺侮，但再要忍受你的侮辱，真是死不瞑目。”

wear out 耗尽；精疲力竭

avenge [ə'ven(d)ʒ] *v.* 替……报仇

gore [gɔː] *v.* 刺伤

assail [ə'seɪl] *v.* 攻击

impunity [ɪm'pjuːnɪtɪ] *n.* 不受惩罚

expire [ɪk'spaɪə] *v.* 死亡

reluctantly [rɪ'lʌktəntlɪ] *adv.* 不情愿地

brook [brʊk] *v.* 忍受

disgrace [dɪs'greɪs] *n.* 耻辱

The Quack Frog
庸医青蛙

读一读，想一想

1. 故事中的青蛙告诉了我们一个什么道理？
2. 你从狐狸的回答中学到了什么样的道理？

精彩故事欣赏

1 A frog once upon a time came forth from his home in the marsh and proclaimed to all the beasts that he was a learned physician, skilled in the use of drugs and able to heal all diseases. A fox asked him, "How can you pretend to prescribe for others, when you are unable to heal your own lame gait and wrinkled skin?"

译　文

1 从前，有一只青蛙，从它沼泽地里的家中出来，对所有的野兽宣告说自己是个博学的医生，善于用药，能医治百病。一只狐狸问它道："你都不能治好你自己跛足的姿势和皱起的皮肤，又怎么能假装给别人开药治病呢？"

阅读无障碍

once upon a time 从前
proclaim [prə'kleɪm] *vt.* 宣告
learned ['lɜːnd] *adj.* 博学的
physician [fɪ'zɪʃ(ə)n] *n.* 医师
skilled [skɪld] *adj.* 有技能的
heal [hiːl] *v.* 治愈
pretend [prɪ'tend] *v.* 假装
prescribe [prɪ'skraɪb] *v.* 开药方

The Swollen Fox
胀肚的狐狸

读一读，想一想

1. 你从这个故事当中学到了什么道理？
2. 同学们自己是否有只看到眼前没想到事后的事情？
3. 现实生活中，同学们该如何避免遇到类似狐狸的状况？

精彩故事欣赏

1 A hungry fox found in a hollow tree a quantity of bread and meat, which some shepherds had placed there against their return. Delighted with his find he slipped in through the narrow aperture and greedily devoured it all. But when he tried to get out again he found himself so swollen after his big meal that he could not squeeze through the hole, and fell to whining and groaning over his misfortune. Another fox, happening to pass that way, came and asked him what the matter was, and, on learning the state of the case, said, "Well, my friend, I see nothing for it but for you

译　文

1 一只饥饿的狐狸在一棵中空的树干中发现了一些牧人保存的面包和肉。高兴之余，狐狸马上挤进那狭窄的树洞，贪婪地狼吞虎咽起来。然而，当他吃完想再出来时，他发现自己的肚子撑得太大，怎么也钻不出原来那个树洞，狐狸便开始呜咽呻吟起自己不幸的遭遇。这时，另一只狐狸恰巧经过，便过去问他是怎么回事。得知来龙去脉后，那只狐狸便

to stay where you are till you shrink to your former size, you'll get out then easily enough."

说道："我的朋友，现在别无他法，你只能待在里边，等到缩回原来的身材，你就能轻松地出来了。"

a quantity of 一些
aperture [ˈæpətʃə] *n.* 穴
devour [dɪˈvaʊə] *v.* 吞食
squeeze [skwiːz] *v.* 挤
whine [waɪn] *v.* 哭诉
groan over [grəʊn] *v.* 呻吟
misfortune [mɪsˈfɔːtʃuːn] *n.* 不幸
shrink [ʃrɪŋk] *v.* 收缩

The Mouse, the Frog, and the Hawk

老鼠、青蛙和老鹰

读一读，想一想

1. 这个故事告诉了我们一个什么道理？
2. 青蛙最终的命运从根本原因上来说是谁导致的？
3. 同学们知道“休戚与共”这个成语的意思吗？

精彩故事欣赏

1 A mouse who always lived on the land, by an unlucky chance formed an intimate acquaintance with a frog, who lived for the most part in the water. The frog, one day intent on mischief, bound the foot of the mouse tightly to his own. Thus joined together, the frog first of all led his friend the mouse to the meadow where they were accustomed to find their food. After this, he gradually led him towards the pool in which he lived, until he reached

译　文

1 一只住在陆地上的老鼠，非常不幸地，和一只大部分时间生活在水里的青蛙结成了好友。有一天，青蛙搞恶作剧，将老鼠的脚紧紧地绑到了自己的脚上，把它们两个连在了一起，青蛙先引老鼠到它们时常觅食的草地上。然后，青蛙慢慢地将老鼠引去自己所住的水

the very brink, when suddenly jumping in he dragged the mouse with him. The frog enjoyed the water amazingly, and swam croaking about, as if he had done a meritorious action. The unhappy mouse was soon suffocated with the water, and his dead body floated about on the surface, tied to the foot of the frog. A hawk observed it, and, pouncing upon it with his talons, carried it up aloft. The frog being still fastened to the leg of the mouse, was also carried off a prisoner, and was eaten by the hawk.

塘，走到水塘边时，青蛙忽然跳了进去，将老鼠也一同拽下了水。青蛙在水里边游边呱呱叫，玩的不亦乐乎，仿佛它做了一件极应称赞的事，不幸的老鼠很快就溺死在水里，它的尸体还仍绑在蛙的脚上，飘浮在水面上。一只老鹰看见了，猛的扑下来，用爪抓起老鼠的尸体就飞了起来，把它带到了半空中。青蛙因为仍绑在老鼠的腿上，也被老鹰俘获，最后进了老鹰的肚子。

阅读无障碍

unlucky [ʌnˈlʌkɪ] *adj.* 不幸的

intimate [ˈɪntɪmət] *adj.* 亲密的

acquaintance [əˈkweɪnt(ə)ns] *n.* 相识

intent [ɪnˈtent] *adj.* 故意的

mischief [ˈmɪstʃɪf] *n.* 恶作剧

tightly [ˈtaɪtlɪ] *adv.* 紧紧地

meadow [ˈmedəʊ] *n.* 草地

amazingly [əˈmezɪŋli] *adv.* 令人惊讶地

croak [krəʊk] *v.* 呱呱地叫

suffocate [ˈsʌfəkeɪt] *v.* 使……窒息

pounce upon 扑向

The Jackdaw and the Pigeons 寒鸦与鸽子

读一读，想一想

1. 这个故事告诉了我们一个什么道理？
2. 同学们知道“偷鸡不成蚀把米”的意思吗？

精彩故事欣赏

1 A jackdaw, watching some pigeons in a farmyard, was filled with envy when he saw how well they were fed, and determined to disguise himself as one of them, in order to secure a share of the good things they enjoyed. So he painted himself white from head to foot and joined the flock, and, so long as he was silent, they never suspected that he was not a pigeon like themselves. But one day he was unwise enough to start chattering, when they at once saw through his disguise and pecked him so unmercifully that he was glad to escape and join his own kind again.

译 文

1 一只寒鸦见农庄里的鸽子吃喝不愁便心生嫉妒，并决意伪装成一只鸽子，以便分享鸽子的食物。于是，寒鸦将自己从头到尾涂成白色并混到鸽子群中，寒鸦一直保持沉默，鸽子们从未怀疑过他不是一只鸽子。可是，有一天，失策的他不小心发出了叫声，鸽子们立即看穿他的伪装，毫不留情地去啄他。寒鸦侥幸逃出了鸽群，回到同类中。然而，因

But the other jackdaws did not recognize him in his white dress, and would not let him feed with them, but drove him away and so he became a homeless wanderer for his pains.

为他的伪装，其它寒鸦都没有认出他来，也不让他同食，而且还赶走他。就这样不幸地，这只寒鸦成了无家可归的流浪鸟。

阅读无障碍

jackdaw [ˈdʒækdɔ] *n.* 寒鸦
pigeon [ˈpɪdʒɪn] *n.* 鸽子
disguise [dɪsˈgaɪz] *v.* 掩饰
flock [flɒk] *n.* 群
silent [ˈsaɪlənt] *adj.* 沉默的
suspect [səˈspekt] *v.* 怀疑
peck [pek] *v.* 啄食
unmercifully [ʌnˈmɝsɪfəli] *adv.* 不仁慈地
wanderer [ˈwɒnd(ə)rə(r)] *n.* 流浪者

The Dog in the Manger

狗占牛槽

读一读，想一想

1. 这个故事告诉了我们一个什么道理？

2. “鸠占鹊巢”是什么意思？

精彩故事欣赏

1 A dog was lying in a manger on the hay which had been put there for the cattle, and when they came and tried to eat, he growled and snapped at them and wouldn't let them get at their food. "What a selfish beast," said one of them to his companions, "he can't eat himself and yet he won't let those eat who can."

译 文

1 一条狗躺在盛着喂牛草料的牛槽中，当牛来到牛槽吃草时，狗冲着他们大吼大叫，不让牛吃草。“好自私的畜生啊！”其中一头牛对同伴说，“他自己不能吃草，还不让能吃的去吃。”

阅读无障碍

manger [ˈmeɪn(d)ʒə] *n.* 马槽

hay [heɪ] *n.* 干草

cattle [ˈkæt(ə)l] *n.* 牛

growl [graʊl] *v.* 咆哮

snap [snæp] *v.* 厉声说

selfish [ˈselfɪʃ] *adj.* 自私的

beast [biːst] *n.* 畜生

companion [kəmˈpænjən] *n.* 同伴

The Oxen and the Axletrees

公牛和车轴

读一读，想一想

1. 这个故事告诉了我们一个什么道理？
2. 如果你是车轴，你会怎么做？

精彩故事欣赏

1 A heavy wagon was being dragged along a country lane by a team of Oxen. The Axletrees groaned and creaked terribly; whereupon the Oxen, turning round, thus addressed the wheels: “Hullo there! why do you make so much noise? We bear all the labor, and we, not you, ought to cry out.”

2 Those who suffer most cry out the least.

译 文

1 几头公牛正使劲拉着沉重的货车行走在乡村小路上，车轴吱嘎吱嘎发出嘈杂的声音，于是公牛回过头对车轮说道：“喂，所有的力都是我们出的，要叫也是我们叫，你叫唤这么大声做什么呢？”

2 那些默不作声的，反而做得最多。

阅读无障碍

wagon ['wæg(ə)n] *n.* 货车

Axletrees [‘æksəltri:] *n.* 轮轴

groan [grəʊn] *v.* 发吱嘎声

creak [kri:k] *v.* 发出咯吱咯吱声

terribly ['terɪblɪ] *adv.* 非常

whereupon [weərə'pɒn] *conj.* 于是

address [ə'dres] *v.* 与……说话

ought [ɔ:t] *aux.* 应该

The Frogs Asking For a King 青蛙求王

读一读，想一想

1. 这个故事告诉了我们一个什么道理？
2. 朱庇特为什么要排苍鹭去给青蛙当国王？

精彩故事欣赏

1 The frogs, grieved at having no established ruler, sent ambassadors to Jupiter entreating for a king. Perceiving their simplicity, he cast down a huge log into the lake. The frogs were terrified at the splash occasioned by its fall and hid themselves in the depths of the pool. But as soon as they realized that the huge log was motionless, they swam again to the top of the water, dismissed their fears, climbed up, and began squatting on it in contempt. After some time they began to think themselves ill-treated in the appointment of so inert a ruler, and sent a second deputation to Jupiter to pray that he would

译　文

1 青蛙们因为没有国王而苦恼不已，于是，他们派代表去拜见朱庇特，请求给他们一个国王。朱庇特看到他们如此蠢笨，便将一截木桩扔进了池塘里。青蛙起初被木桩落水溅起的水声吓了一大跳，立刻都躲到池塘深处去了。但后来当青蛙发现木头不会动时，他们又游出水面来，觉得木头没什么可怕的，并爬上木桩，蔑视地坐在木桩上。过了段时间，青蛙觉得朱庇特指派

set over them another sovereign. He then gave them an eel to govern them. When the frogs discovered his easy good nature, they sent yet a third time to Jupiter to beg him to choose for them still another king. Jupiter, displeased with all their complaints, sent a heron, who preyed upon the frogs day by day till there were none left to croak upon the lake.

他们这样一个呆滞的国王亏待了他们，于是又派人去见朱庇特，请求给他们换一个国王。朱庇特就又派了鳝鱼去给他们当国王。当青蛙们发现鳝鱼性格随和好糊弄之后，又第三次派人去就请求朱庇特选派另外一个国王。朱庇特对他们一而再再而三的抱怨感到十分生气，便派了一只苍鹭到他们那里去，苍鹭每天都捕食青蛙结果青蛙都被吃光了，也没有青蛙能够再继续呱呱的抱怨了。

阅读无障碍

grieve [griːv] *v.* 苦恼
ambassador [æmˈbæsədə] *n.* 代表
entreat [ɪnˈtriːt] *v.* 请求
perceive [pəˈsiːv] *v.* 察觉
occasion [əˈkeɪʒ(ə)n] *v.* 引起
motionless [ˈməʊʃnləs] *adj.* 静止的
dismiss [dɪsˈmɪs] *v.* 解散
deputation [depjʊˈteɪʃ(ə)n] *n.* 代表团
sovereign [ˈsɒvrɪn] *n.* 君主

The Olive-Tree and the Fig-Tree

橄榄树与无花果树

读一读，想一想

1. 这个故事告诉了我们一个什么道理？
2. 通过这个故事，你在自己的生活、学习中应该如何做？

精彩故事欣赏

1 An olive tree and a fig tree were talking one winter day.

2 "I feel sorry for you," said the olive tree, "Every year you lose all your leaves and have to shiver through the winter with bare branches. But I stay green and beautiful all the year round. Still, I suppose we can't all be good-looking."

3 The fig tree was silent. Later that day the weather turned very cold. Great grey clouds filled the sky and it was very still. It began to snow heavily.

4 All that night it snowed, and all the

译文

1 一个冬日，橄榄树和无花果树聊起天来。

2 "你真可怜，"橄榄树说，"每年冬天，你的叶子都会掉光，只剩下光秃秃的树枝，在寒冬中瑟瑟发抖。可我一年四季都郁郁葱葱、漂漂亮亮。当然了，不是所有人都能这样美的。"

3 无花果树沉默无语。那天晚些时候，天变得很冷。天空布满了大片乌云，

next day. Fields and hedges were thickly covered and people had to dig paths from their houses to the roadside. The snow settled on the olive tree, drifting in little piles in the leaves, weighing down the branches so that they snapped and fell to the white ground below. The fig tree was more fortunate. She had no leaves to trap the snow and it drifted harmlessly through the bare twigs.

5 When the thaw came she was still standing, ready to put out her new spring leaves, but the olive tree lay broken, a twisted jumble of sticks and brown leaves.

万籁俱寂，天开始下起大雪。

4 雪整整下了一个晚上，第二天又下了一整天。田野和树篱都覆盖了一层厚厚的雪，人们只好从家门口挖出一条条小路通往路边。雪花落在橄榄树上，一点点地堆积在叶片上，树枝被压弯了，最后折断了，掉落在白色的雪地上。无花果树比较幸运，她没有叶子，挡不住雪，雪从光秃秃的嫩枝间飘过，丝毫没有损害到树。

5 积雪融化了，无花果树依然挺立，准备一到春天，就吐露新芽，长出嫩叶；而橄榄树却被压断了，成为一堆乱糟糟的残枝败叶。

阅读无障碍

olive [ˈɒlɪv] *n.* 橄榄

fig [fɪg] *n.* 无花果

shiver [ˈʃɪvə] *v.* 颤抖

bare [beə] *adj.* 空的

still [stɪl] *adj.* 寂静的

drift [drɪft] *v.* 漂移

weigh [weɪ] *v.* 重荷

twig [twɪg] *n.* 小枝

twist [twɪst] *v.* 拧

jumble [ˈdʒʌmb(ə)l] *n.* 混乱

The Lion and the Boar
狮子和野猪

读一读，想一想

1. 这个故事告诉了我们一个什么道理？

2. 你知道“鹬蚌相争渔翁得利”这个成语的故事吗？请解释它的意思。

精彩故事欣赏

1 On a summer day, when the great heat induced a general thirst among the beasts, a lion and a boar came at the same moment to a small well to drink. They fiercely disputed which of them should drink first, and were soon engaged in the agonies of a mortal combat. When they stopped suddenly to catch their breath for a fiercer renewal of the fight, they saw some vultures waiting in the distance to feast on the one that should fall first. They at once made up their quarrel, saying, “It is better for us to make friends, than to become the food of crows or vultures.”

译　文

1 一个炎热的夏天，酷暑让百兽们都口干舌燥，一头狮子和一头野猪同时来到一口小井喝水。他们为谁先喝水激烈的争吵起来，很快他们便陷入了一场殊死搏斗中。当他们停下来喘口气以再次投入更为凶狠的战斗中时，他们看到几只秃鹫站在不远处，等着吃掉这场搏斗中的败者。他们马上和解，说道：“与其打输果腹乌鸦秃鹫，我们还不如休战成为朋友呢！”

induce [ɪnˈdjuːs] *v.* 引起

fiercely [ˈfɪəslɪ] *adv.* 猛烈地

dispute [dɪˈspjuːt] *n.* 争吵

combat [ˈkɒmbæt] *n.* 战斗

catch one's breath 歇口气

renewal [rɪˈnjuːəl] *n.* 更新

vulture [ˈvʌltʃə] *n.* 秃鹰

feast [fiːst] *v.* 享受

The Walnut-Tree
核桃树

读一读，想一想

1. 核桃树为什么抱怨？
2. 这个故事告诉了我们一个什么道理？

精彩故事欣赏

1 A walnut tree standing by the roadside bore an abundant crop of fruit. For the sake of the nuts, the passers-by broke its branches with stones and sticks. The walnut-Tree piteously exclaimed, "O wretched me! That those whom I cheer with my fruit should repay me with these painful requitals!"

译 文

1 路旁长着一棵核桃树，树上结满核桃，路过的人们都用石头和木棍朝着树枝打，以此获取核桃。可怜的核桃树暗自神伤，抱怨道："我真是太倒霉了！我把果实提供给人们，换来的却是这样痛苦的回报。"

阅读无障碍

abundant [ə'bʌndənt] *adj.* 大量的
for the sake of 为了
passer-by ['pɑːsə baɪ] *n.* 过路人
piteously ['pɪtɪəslɪ] *adv.* 可怜地
repay [rɪ'peɪ] *v.* 回报
requital [rɪ'kwaɪtl] *n.* 报酬

The Tortoise and the Eagle
乌龟和老鹰

读一读，想一想

1. 这个故事告诉了我们一个什么道理？
2. 通过学习这个故事，对你在日后的生活有什么启示？

精彩故事欣赏

1 A tortoise, lazily basking in the sun, complained to the sea-birds of her hard fate, that no one would teach her to fly. An eagle, hovering near, heard her lamentation and demanded what reward she would give him if he would take her aloft and float her in the air. "I will give you," she said, "all the riches of the Red Sea." "I will teach you to fly then," said the eagle, and taking her up in his talons he carried her almost to the clouds suddenly he let her go, and she fell on a lofty mountain, dashing her shell to pieces. The tortoise exclaimed in the moment of death: "I have deserved my present fate, for what had I to do with

译 文

1 一只乌龟一边懒洋洋地晒着太阳，一边向海鸟哭诉自己命运坎坷，说没有人教她飞翔。一只盘旋在附近的老鹰听到她的诉苦，便问如果带她到空中飞翔，她愿意给予什么奖赏。乌龟说："我愿给你红海中所有的财宝"。老鹰说："那么我就教你飞吧"。说罢，鹰爪抓起乌龟带她飞到空中直冲进云霄，突然鹰爪一放，乌龟摔落到一座高山上，龟壳跌得粉碎。临死之际乌龟悲叹到：

wings and clouds, who can with difficulty move about on the earth? "

"这是我应得的报应！我在地面上行动都很困难了，为什么还想飞到云端里去呢？"

阅读无障碍

tortoise [ˈtɔːtəs] *n.* 乌龟
bask [bɑːsk] *v.* 晒太阳
hover [ˈhɒvə(r)] *v.* 盘旋
lamentation [ˌlæmənˈteɪʃn] *n.* 悲叹
aloft [əˈlɒft] *adv.* 在空中
lofty [ˈlɒfti] *adj.* 高耸的
dash [dæʃ] *v.* 猛撞
deserve [dɪˈzɜːv] *v.* 应受

The Kid on the Housetop

站在屋顶的小山羊与狼

读一读，想一想

1. 这个故事告诉了我们一个什么道理？

2. 你能否从正反两方面来看待小山羊咒骂狼的行为？这两方面是什么？

精彩故事欣赏

1 A kid was perched up on the top of a house, and looking down saw a wolf passing under him. Immediately he began to revile and attack his enemy. "Murderer and thief," he cried, "Why are you here near honest folks' houses? How dare you make an appearance where your vile deeds are known?"

2 "Curse away, my young friend," said the wolf. "It is easy to be brave from a safe distance."

译 文

1 一只在屋顶上歇息的小山羊，低头刚好看到一头狼经过屋下。小山羊马上破口辱骂到："你这个凶手、小偷，这里都是老实人住的地方，你来这里干什么？你的卑鄙行径大家都已经知道了，你怎么还敢出现在这里？"

2 狼说道："你就骂吧，小东西，躲在安全的地方逞英雄再容易不过了。"

阅读无障碍

perch [pɜːtʃ] *v.* 栖息

immediately [ɪˈmiːdɪətlɪ] *adv.* 立即

revile [rɪˈvaɪl] *v.* 辱骂

folk [fəʊk] *n.* 人们

make an appearance 出现

vile [vaɪl] *adj.* 卑鄙的

curse [kɜːs] *v.* 诅咒

distance [ˈdɪst(ə)ns] *n.* 远方

The Fox without a Tail
断尾巴狐狸

读一读，想一想

1. 这个故事告诉了我们一个什么道理？
2. 狐狸的行为，你怎么看待？

精彩故事欣赏

1 A fox's tail was caught in a trap. When he was trying to release himself, he lost his whole tail except the stump.

2 At first he was ashamed to see the other foxes because he had no tail, but he was determined to face his misfortune. He called all the foxes to a meeting.

3 When they had gotten together, the fox said that they should all do away with their tails.

4 He said that their tails were very inconvenient when they met with their enemies.

5 He did not talk about any

译　文

1 一只狐狸的尾巴被夹住了，当他试着挣脱时，整条尾巴都被挣断了。

2 起初，他因为自己没有尾巴看到其他狐狸就会觉得羞愧，但后来，他决定直面自己的不幸，就召集了所有的狐狸开会。

3 大家到齐后，狐狸说大家都应该割掉尾巴。

4 他说尾巴在遭遇敌人时很不方便。

5 他没说尾巴的任何好

advantages of the tail. “You are right,” said one of the older foxes, “but I don’t think you would advise us to do away with our tails if you hadn’t lost it yourself first.”

处。一只老狐狸说到：“你说的对，但如果你没失去你的尾巴，你才不会劝大家去割尾巴。”

阅读无障碍

trap [træp] *n.* 陷阱
release [rɪˈliːs] *v.* 释放
stump [stʌmp] *n.* 残余部分
ashamed [əˈʃeɪmd] *adj.* 惭愧的
misfortune [mɪsˈfɔːtʃuːn] *n.* 不幸
do away with 去掉
inconvenient [ɪnkənˈviːnɪənt] *adj.* 不便的
advantage [ədˈvɑːntɪdʒ] *n.* 优点

The Vain Jackdaw
爱慕虚荣的寒鸦

读一读，想一想

1. 乌鸦为什么要插上别的鸟儿的羽毛？
2. 从这个故事当中你受到什么启发？

精彩故事欣赏

1 Jupiter determined, it is said, to create a sovereign over the birds, and made proclamation that, on a certain day, they should all present themselves before him, when he would himself choose the most beautiful among them to be king. The jackdaw, knowing his own ugliness, searched through the woods and fields, and collected the feathers which had fallen from the wings of his companions, and stuck them in all parts of his body, hoping thereby to make himself the most beautiful of all. When the appointed day arrived, and the birds had assembled before Jupiter,

译　文

1 据说，朱庇特决定立一个君主来统治鸟类，于是便公布了个日子，令所有的鸟来面见他，届时他将亲自选出最美的鸟儿为王。鸦深知自己容貌丑陋，遍寻森林和田野，搜集了同伴掉落的羽毛粘到自己身上，借此希望把自己变成最美的鸟儿。到了指定的日子，所有的鸟儿齐聚在宙斯面前，寒鸦也穿着多羽华服出现了。朱庇特见他羽毛华丽，便要封它

the jackdaw also made his appearance in his many-feathered finery. On Jupiter proposing to make him king, on account of the beauty of his plumage, the birds indignantly protested, and each plucking from him his own feathers, the jackdaw was again nothing but a Jackdaw.

为王，众鸟愤慨抗议，把自己的羽毛从寒鸦身上拔下来，于是寒鸦原形毕露了。

阅读无障碍

sovereign ['sɒvrɪn] *n.* 君主

proclamation [prɒklə'meɪʃn] *adj.* 冻结的

present [pri'z(ə)nt] *v.* 呈现

ugliness ['ʌglɪnɪs] *n.* 丑陋

stick [stɪk] *v.* 粘贴

assemble [ə'semb(ə)l] *v.* 集合；聚集

finery ['faɪn(ə)rɪ] *n.* 华丽的服饰

plumage ['pluːmɪdʒ] *n.* 翅膀

indignantly [in'dignəntli] *adv.* 愤怒地

pluck [plʌk] *v.* 拔

The Wild Boar and the Fox

野猪与狐狸

读一读，想一想

1. 野猪为什么要在没有危险的时候磨牙？
2. 你是一个未雨绸缪的人吗？

精彩故事欣赏

1 A wild boar stood under a tree and rubbed his tusks against the trunk. A fox passing by asked him why he thus sharpened his teeth when there was no danger threatening from either huntsman or hound. He replied, "I do it advisedly, for it would never do to have to sharpen my weapons just at the time I ought to be using them."

译文

1 有头野猪站在树下靠着树干磨獠牙。狐狸路过问到，这里没有猎人或猎犬，为什么要磨牙呢。野猪回答道："我这样做是经过深思熟虑的，因为一旦危险降临我要用到獠牙的时候，就没有磨牙的工夫了。"

阅读无障碍

rub [rʌb] *v.* 擦

tusk [tʌsk] *n.* 长牙

trunk [trʌŋk] *n.* 树干

thus [ðʌs] *adv.* 因此

sharpen [ˈʃɑːp(ə)n] *v.* 磨快

either… or… 或者……或者……

advisedly [ədˈvaɪzɪdlɪ] *adv.* 经过考虑地

weapon [ˈwep(ə)n] *n.* 武器

The Fawn and His Mother

小鹿和妈妈

读一读，想一想

1. 鹿妈妈有那么多的优势，可她为什么还是怕狗呢？
2. 这个故事中，你得到了什么启发？

精彩故事欣赏

1 A young fawn once said to his mother, "You are larger than a dog, and swifter, and more used to running, and you have your horns as a defense; why, then, O mother! do the hounds frighten you so?" She smiled, and said: "I know full well, my son, that all you say is true. I have the advantages you mention, but when I hear even the bark of a single dog I feel ready to faint, and fly away as fast as I can."

译　文

1 一只年轻的小鹿有一次问他的妈妈："你比狗的体型大，比他敏捷，而且更惯于奔跑，并且你的犄角可以用来防御；可是妈妈，为什么你这么害怕猎犬呢？"鹿妈妈笑了笑说："我的儿子啊，我知道你说的全是事实。你说的优势我全有，但是即便是一只狗的吠声都要把我吓晕了，所以我只能尽我所能的跑快。"

fawn [fɔːn] *n.* 小鹿

swift [swɪft] *adj.* 敏捷的

horn [hɔːn] *n.* 犄角

defense [dɪˈfens] *n.* 防御

frighten [ˈfraɪt(ə)n] *v.* 惊吓

advantage [ədˈvɑːntɪdʒ] *n.* 优势

bark [bɑːk] *n.* 狗叫

faint [feɪnt] *v.* 昏倒

The Fox and the Lion

狐狸和狮子

读一读，想一想

1. 这个故事告诉了我们一个什么道理？
2. 如果你是狐狸，你会怎么做？

精彩故事欣赏

1 When a fox who had never yet seen a lion, fell in with him by chance for the first time in the forest, he was so frightened that he nearly died with fear. On meeting him for the second time, he was still much alarmed, but not to the same extent as at first. On seeing him the third time, he so increased in boldness that he went up to him and commenced a familiar conversation with him.

2 Acquaintance softens prejudices.

译 文

1 一只从未与狮子谋面的狐狸，第一次偶然在森林里碰见狮子时，几乎吓得魂飞魄散。第二次见到狮子，他依然惊恐不已，但已经比第一次镇定了。狐狸第三次碰见狮子，他的胆子大了些，径直走上前去与狮子展开了一段亲切的谈话。

2 熟识淡化了偏见。

阅读无障碍

by chance 偶然地

fear [fɪə] *adj.* 冻结的

alarm [ə'lɑːm] *v.* 使惊恐

boldness ['boldnɪs] *n.* 大胆

commence [kə'mens] *v.* 开始

acquaintance [ə'kweɪnt(ə)ns] *n.* 相识

soften ['sɒf(ə)n] *v.* 使缓和

prejudice ['predʒʊdɪs] *n.* 偏见

The Stag at the Pool

池边的雄鹿

读一读，想一想

1. 是什么原因导致雄鹿被狮子抓到？
2. 从这个故事当中你受到什么启发？

精彩故事欣赏

1 A stag overpowered by heat came to a spring to drink. Seeing his own shadow reflected in the water, he greatly admired the size and variety of his horns, but felt angry with himself for having such slender and weak feet. While he was thus contemplating himself, a lion appeared at the pool and crouched to spring upon him. The stag immediately took to flight, and exerting his utmost speed, as long as the plain was smooth and open kept himself easily at a safe distance from the lion. But entering a wood he became entangled by his horns, and the lion quickly came up

译　文

1 一头雄鹿难耐酷暑来到泉边喝水。看到水中倒映出自己健美的体魄、漂亮的犄角，雄鹿顾影自怜起来，但又对自己细弱的四肢而愤愤不平。正在他沉思之际，一头狮子悄悄来到水边扑向了他。雄鹿马上飞速逃了起来，在平坦开阔的平地上雄鹿跟狮子保持着安全的距离。但当他跑进森林后，他的犄角就被树林缠绕住了，狮子很快就赶上并抓住

to him and caught him. When too late, he thus reproached himself: “Woe is me! How I have deceived myself! These feet which would have saved me I despised, and I gloried in these antlers which have proved my destruction.”

What is most truly valuable is often underrated.

了雄鹿。为时已晚之际，雄鹿自责到：“悲乎哀哉；我怎自欺到这般！本可救我性命的四肢，我不屑一顾；一直洋洋得意的犄角，却送我性命。”

最为珍贵的东西往往被人轻贱。

阅读无障碍

overpower [əʊvə'paʊə] *adj.* 僵硬地
shadow ['ʃædəʊ] *n.* 影子
reflect [rɪ'flekt] *v.* 反射
slender ['slendə] *adj.* 细长的
contemplate ['kɒntempleɪt] *v.* 沉思
crouch [kraʊtʃ] *v.* 蹲伏
exert [ɪg'zɜːt] *v.* 发挥
entangle [ɪn'tæŋg(ə)l] *v.* 使纠缠
reproach [rɪ'prəʊtʃ] *v.* 责备
deceive [dɪ'siːv] *v.* 欺骗
despise [dɪ'spaɪz] *v.* 轻视
glory ['glɔːrɪ] *v.* 自豪
underrate [ʌndə'reɪt] *v.* 低估

The Dog and the Shadow

叼着肉的狗

读一读，想一想

1. 狗本来已经有一块肉了，是因为什么导致他最后又没肉了？
2. 这个故事告诉了我们一个什么道理？

精彩故事欣赏

1 A dog, crossing a bridge over a stream with a piece of flesh in his mouth, saw his own shadow in the water and took it for that of another dog, with a piece of meat double his own in size. He immediately let go of his own, and fiercely attacked the other dog to get his larger piece from him. He thus lost both: that which he grasped at in the water, because it was a shadow, and his own, because the stream swept it away.

译　文

1 一条狗叼着肉过河，走到桥上看见水中自己的倒影，误以为是另一条狗叼着比自己口中两倍大的肉。他马上放开嘴里的肉扑到水里去抢那块更大的肉。结果，他两块肉都没得到，水中那块肉本来就只是倒影，而他原有那块肉也被河水冲走了。

阅读无障碍

stream [striːm] *n.* 溪流

flesh [fleʃ] *n.* 肉

take …for…. 把……认作……；误认为……

let go of… 放开

fiercely [ˈfɪəslɪ] *adv.* 猛烈地

thus [ðʌs] *adv.* 因此

grasp [grɑːsp] *v.* 抓住

sweep…away 卷走

The Mice and the Weasels

老鼠和黄鼠狼

读一读，想一想

1. 你认为老鼠应该怎么做？
2. 这个故事告诉我们什么道理？

精彩故事欣赏

1 The weasels and the mice waged a perpetual war with each other, in which much blood was shed. The weasels were always the victors. The mice thought that the cause of their frequent defeats was that they had no leaders set apart from the general army to command them, and that they were exposed to dangers from lack of discipline. They therefore chose as leaders mice that were most renowned for their family descent, strength, and counsel, as well as those most noted for their courage in the fight, so that they might be better marshaled in battle array and formed into

译 文

1 黄鼠狼和老鼠之间的仗打得无休无止，流了不少血。每一次都是黄鼠狼获胜。老鼠认为，它们屡战屡败的原因是它们没有领袖来统领大军，由于缺乏训练，时常处于危险的境地。因此它们挑选出具有家世显赫、力量强大、足智多谋、战斗勇敢的老鼠将它们排成更好的战队，组成小队、联队和大队。一切都已完备，军队训练完毕，传令的老鼠便及

troops, regiments, and battalions. When all this was done, and the army disciplined, and the herald mouse had duly proclaimed war by challenging the weasels, the newly chosen generals bound their heads with straws, that they might be more conspicuous to all their troops. Scarcely had the battle begun, when a great rout overwhelmed the mice, who scampered off as fast as they could to their holes. The generals, not being able to get in on account of the ornaments on their heads, were all captured and eaten by the weasels.

时向黄鼠狼宣战。新选的将领老鼠们在脑袋上系上稻草，这样它们在老鼠大军中就更加显眼。战争刚刚开始，老鼠又大败，它们拼命地逃回洞里。那些将领因为头上装饰着高冠根本进不了洞，最后全被黄鼠狼俘虏并吃掉了。

阅读无障碍

frequent [ˈfriːkwənt] *adj.* 频繁的

discipline [ˈdisiplin] *n.* 训练

therefore [ˈðeəfɔː] *adv.* 因此

renowned [riˈnaund] *a.* 有名的

descent [diˈsent] *n.* 家世

counsel [ˈkaunsəl] *n.* 商议

herald [ˈherəld] *n.* 先驱

conspicuous [kənˈspikjuəs] *adj.* 显著的

The Bear and the Fox

熊与狐狸

读一读，想一想

1. 你认为狐狸是仁慈的吗？
2. 这个故事告诉我们什么道理？

精彩故事欣赏

1 A bear boasted very much of his philanthropy, saying that of all animals he was the most tender in his regard for man, for he had such respect for him that he would not even touch his dead body. A fox hearing these words said with a smile to the bear, "Oh! That you would eat the dead and not the living."

译 文

1 一只熊在吹嘘自己的仁慈，说："所有的动物中，只有熊对人最仁爱，它很敬重人，连人的尸体也不去碰一下。" 一只狐狸听到这些话，微笑地对熊说："噢，那你还是吃死人吧，别生吃活人了。"

阅读无障碍

boast [bəʊst] *v.* 夸口说
philanthropy [fɪˈlænθrəpɪ] *n.* 慈善
tender [ˈtendə] *adj.* 温柔的
in regard for 关于
respect [rɪˈspekt] *n.* 尊重